AN ALPHABET OF
ATTRIBUTES

AN ALPHABET OF ATTRIBUTES

ASPECTS OF
HUMAN THOUGHT AND CONDUCT

BY

HAROLD DOWNS

Essay Index Reprint Series

originally published by

SIR ISAAC PITMAN & SONS, LTD.

BOOKS FOR LIBRARIES PRESS
FREEPORT, NEW YORK

First Published 1931
Reprinted 1970

STANDARD BOOK NUMBER:
8369-1498-8

LIBRARY OF CONGRESS CATALOG CARD NUMBER:
72-107695

PRINTED IN THE UNITED STATES OF AMERICA

FOREWORD

It is, I believe, the main object of Mr. Downs to excite in the reader of these pages the desire to read and think; to persuade him at least to think, even if he does not always understand. I believe this is a commendable object, and I hope it will be achieved.

It will be a good thing for the reader if he will think long and carefully over every one of the many interesting points to which his attention is directed. The reader may, as a result of this, come to the conclusion that there are many things that are true even though they are beyond his understanding. There are far too many readers nowadays who do not get beyond the mere printed word. They do not unpack the parcel to see what it contains, and their reading is more or less useless in consequence of this omission.

Mr. Downs's effort will not have been in vain if he succeeds in inducing the reader of this book to exercise his mind and brain in serious thought of the serious things presented to him for consideration, and it will not, from this point of view, matter very much whether he agrees or disagrees with the views and conclusions put before him.

I heartily applaud Mr. Downs's motive in collecting and presenting to us the reflections of his leisure moments, and I wish the book the success which it undoubtedly deserves.

JAMES HYNES.

PREFACE

THIS book by my fellow-townsman, Mr. Harold Downs, is an anthology. The flowers of thought, culled here and there from innumerable writers, are brought together by the author with comments of his own clearly and modestly stated. It is not a book to read at a sitting, but a vade-mecum. With the author we wander through an alphabet beginning with Adaptability and ending with Zeal. This anthology might have been entitled "Revaluations," because ordinary values accepted by the average man or woman in the street are here revalued not in a didactic spirit but tentatively. The author lays great stress throughout on the necessity of attempting to know oneself before one accepts the knowledge of others.

First and last this book is subjective in the sense that observation of what lies without must be quickened by observation of what is within. The author makes it plain that it takes more courage to confront ourselves than to confront others. To look first, to weigh the possible consequences, and then to leap is the act of a truly brave man.

Right revaluations on the part of the Individual would have immediate repercussions on the Crowd. To-day the *vox populi* is too vocal, and much too insistent. And yet, in sharpest contrast, publicity is given in fullest measure to personality. Any outstanding figure is "featured." The many are, perhaps, beginning to understand the few after centuries of misunderstanding. It is obvious that the author of this book belongs to the few who not only think for themselves but are able to make others think. This alphabet from A to Z is thought-inspired and thought-inspiring.

Oddly enough, Mr. Downs, dealing in a catholic spirit with so much, has left out both mirth and humour. And he forbears to use a publicist's most trenchant weapon—ridicule. Admittedly, it is a dangerous weapon, like irony, but I think he could use it with advantage. Again and again, in my own experience, I have found that it is a waste of breath to tell a young man or woman that what they may propose to do is unwise; but if I can hint discreetly that he or she is likely to become a target for ridicule, I am confident of making an impression. Ridicule is certainly the only weapon that can deal effectively with those diabolical twins: conceit and ignorance.

I have read this alphabet with the greatest interest and can commend it wholeheartedly.

HORACE ANNESLEY VACHELL.

CONTENTS

PAGE

FOREWORD . . . v

PREFACE . . . vii

INTRODUCTION . . xi

NO.		PAGE	NO.		PAGE
1.	ADAPTABILITY	1	14.	NERVOUSNESS .	96
2.	BRAVERY . .	7	15.	OBSERVATION .	103
3.	CHARITY . .	13	16.	PREJUDICE .	111
4.	DETERMINATION	19	17.	QUEERNESS .	119
5.	EFFORT . .	26	18.	RESISTANCE .	127
6.	FAITH . . .	33	19.	SINCERITY .	135
7.	GENEROSITY .	42	20.	TACT . . .	142
8.	HAPPINESS .	51	21.	UNDERSTANDING	149
9.	IMAGINATION .	59	22.	VERSATILITY .	157
10.	JEALOUSY . .	66	23.	WISDOM . .	165
11.	KINDNESS . .	73	24.	XENOMANIA .	174
12.	LOVE . . .	80	25.	YOUTHFULNESS	184
13.	MODESTY . .	88	26.	ZEAL . . .	191

CONCLUSION 199

QUOTATIONS : AUTHORS 201

BOOKS 203

INTRODUCTION

THE *Oxford English Dictionary* contains a record of 414,825 words; Shakespeare drew upon only 15,000, and his vocabulary was abnormally extensive. For most of us a few thousands suffice. Words are counters, but we use many of them without full understanding of the ideas that bring them into currency.

My *Alphabet of Attributes*, perhaps with one exception, is composed of words that are part of any averagely intelligent adult's working vocabulary. Reflection on any one of them gives scope for speculative thought, which, rightly exercised, must deepen understanding.

Samuel Johnson has it that so many objections might be made to everything that nothing could overcome them but the necessity of doing something. The something that I have attempted to do is to stimulate my own thought on aspects of life merely to help self-understanding. I have not tried to theorize or to work out a philosophy of life. My thoughts, for what they are worth, if anything, have been set down in sincerity and, I hope, without dogmatism.

Self-analysis and self-revelation should be part

of the expression of the life of any individual. Realization of this fact is my excuse for working through an alphabet of my own making, the better to learn my own reactions to thoughts that are often firmly linked with actions.

HAROLD DOWNS

AN ALPHABET OF ATTRIBUTES

ADAPTABILITY

LIFE is a series of adjustments. We enter the world with influences and tendencies that are the gifts of heredity, and we pass through life unable to escape from the ever-present and ever-pressing effects of environment. Before the dawn of consciousness, environment begins to play its part. There is a point of illumination in the lives of all who endeavour to order living on a plane of intelligence. One writer, Mr. Edgar James Swift, has it that to adjust oneself quickly and successfully to new and changing conditions is probably the best single statement of intelligence. To envisage that point early in life and to keep it truly focused are aims of primary importance in any sound scheme of self-development. In practicality what happens before these aims are realized are happenings that cannot be related to self-responsibility.

Heredity may bestow enormous, even unique, advantages. On the other hand, it may impose permanent handicaps. If we are fortunate, the advantages will reveal themselves in Nature's appointed ways, and if we are unfortunate we shall, in similar manner, sooner or later be brought face to face with the handicaps. None the less, there is not the same inevitability about the effect of heredity as there is about the instinctive desire to live once we are born. If there were, fatalism would be our inseparable, though not necessarily our welcome, companion from the dawn of life to death itself.

Environment and Its Influences.

Environment gives us our touchstone of reality, endows us with the power to make dark places light, and renders possible the captaincy of the vessel, the body and mind, through the instrumentality of which we become aware of spirit, the vessel upon which life's journey is made. It is, however, impossible for us to control, useless for us to worry about, the environmental influences that mould us before we attain senior rank. The food we eat, the prayers we say, nay the prayers that are said for us, the things we are taught, the duties that are imposed upon us— these and many other features of our early days are inescapable experiences because they are introduced into our lives by others over whom we have no control. But when we reach years of discretion, or, by no means synonymous, when we to some extent become the dictators of our own activities, we ourselves introduce, consciously and unconsciously, manifold influences into our lives. From that time onwards an increasing adaptability can wisely be regarded as a stern necessity. Environment constantly changes. Adaptability is the reflection of change. We must relate ourselves to people and things alike. We cannot go through life as isolated units. We cannot remain indifferent to the impersonal. To make the attempt to live hermitically would be to emphasize the need for adaptability. The hermit's life is intensely individualized. He must do all, in conjunction with Nature, for himself. As ordinary members of civilized society, much is done for us. Our individual responsibility is often merely to adapt ourselves to the requirements of custom, convention, social requirement, civic obligation. The impress of the impersonal is felt when we encounter the "atmosphere" of environment. Who, for example, has not been impressed by the "atmosphere," not climatic, but spiritual, of the interior of a cathedral?

The Mainspring of Adaptability.

The mainspring of adaptability should be principle, though some of the mechanism will be linked with practicality, expediency, the common sense of living, the nonsense of leisure. What we think ought to be done is not always what we do because we are humans and as such must fall short of the ideal. Nevertheless, idealistic thought and attempts to translate it in terms of everyday life are some of the means by which we develop on sound lines. They help us to keep life in true perspective. Impelled to handle circumstances, we need to know not only the best methods to adapt ourselves to them, but what constitutes the best adaptation. Thus we learn through self-discovery.

Discovery of Self.

"To discover ourselves," states Professor E. T. Campagnac, M.A., in *Education*, "is to learn that we possess and can use powers with which we had hardly credited ourselves, and have weaknesses which we certainly had not suspected; it is to find ourselves strangely different from what we had supposed we were, and to find the world both more friendly and more difficult, both more hospitable and more hostile, both more intelligent and more stupid, than we imagined it could be. We perceive that we want new things, some of which the world readily grants while it withholds others, and that of the things which we have already known the need some are much harder to get than we thought when we received them at the hands of the guardians of our earlier years,

4

perhaps even without asking for them." In these interestingly varied learning processes we discover ourselves and face realities. Here, ready adaptation to circumstances will be best; there, to resist adaptation will be the only way to further worthwhile achievement. Sometimes the ideal and practical readily blend; sometimes they are in stern antagonism. To adapt ourselves to the discomforts of bare necessity because misuse of material luxury can, and often does, deaden the spirit, is as prejudicial as is adaptation to hindering and hampering conditions that are removable by well-directed, soundly planned efforts, rigorously maintained by the unshakable determination to advance ourselves physically, intellectually, and spiritually.

Attributes as Signposts.

We need to have clear ideas of attributes, good and evil, as companions on our march through life. They are signposts. They indicate the way. Whatever the way is, to pursue it involves either adaptation to the forces that impinge upon us or resistance to the forces, which resistance creates new forces, adaptation to which can be readily made because of its beneficial effects. If we consciously try to find out what it is best for us to do or to refrain from doing, adaptation or non-adaptation to the facts of life as they present themselves does not constitute a problem for us. We know what we ought to try to do and we try to do it. To cultivate and to extend a sound degree of adaptability enables us to see truth and to increase the capacity to be true to self, without which truth we must ever remain strangers to human attributes of great worth.

BRAVERY

IT is easy to define Bravery too narrowly. A man does a spectacular act—saves a life at great risk to his own—and it is brought to the notice of millions of readers in these days of the popular Press. He probably is a brave man, but the brave act that he has done on the spur of the moment does not necessarily demand the quality of bravery that must be demonstrated by thousands of men and women to make life tolerable for them. Think of bravery in another connexion. We often associate it with the battlefield, and those who have read Remarque's powerful war story, *All Quiet on the Western Front*, or the companion war play, *Journey's End*, by R. C. Sherriff, will find in either of these books abundant material to prove the contention that modern warfare calls for individual bravery. Nevertheless, there are brave acts done in battle that are the outcome of reaction to circumstances that are separable from bravery.

Modern study of crowd psychology has taught us many lessons. The soldier, who, with his fighting colleagues, goes into action, can more readily respond to the word of command as one of many within the sphere of danger than commit an act that runs counter to the many that are being done simultaneously near him. The man or woman in a theatre who will deliberately shout "bosh" when all around are highly appreciative of the performance is uncommon. In one case, action is with the general current of thought and action; in the other it is against it. This makes a big difference. Recognition of this fact does not, of course, contain even the germ of a suggestion that modern warfare does not involve the fighters in participation in numerous situations in which bravery must be displayed for life to be saved. But soldiers, during a war, live abnormal lives. Let us think of bravery as it finds expression in the common life during times of peace.

Tests of Character.

When we want to pay tribute to a man's bravery we sometimes say that he is "as brave as a lion." It is one of those sayings that come trippingly off the tongue and that are more picturesque than truthful. A compliment is intended. To tell the man that he is "as brave as a pig or a fox," or even a "timid sheep," would probably be regarded as an insult. In rock bottom fact it would be a truer compliment than when he is "lionized" in this rather than in the dictionary sense of the word, for any one of the three animals mentioned, taking size, strength, weight, and natural fighting abilities into account, is braver than the lion. The brave are the courageous, the fearless, the gallant.

Courage, fearlessness, and gallantry are qualities that each of us reveal in daily life to a greater or less extent. The common round, "the trivial task," are often rigorous tests of character. They constitute life in its varied manifestations. It is the attitude that we adopt towards them that brings out the qualities of character. To resolve to live life in splendid isolation might reflect one expression of bravery, but it would be blind. We have to live with, and move among, our fellow creatures. It is living and moving that often call for bravery. Goethe, recalls Sir John Adams, M.A., B.Sc., LL.D., in *Educational Theories*, "has a couplet that almost every German schoolmaster used to make his pupils learn by heart. Its translation runs : 'A talent may be cultivated in solitude, but a character needs the whirl of the world.' Man is, as Aristotle told us long ago, a sociable animal, meant to live in communities, and unable to attain his full development apart from his fellows. The solitary man is not a real man. He must either be a superman and rise to the status of godhood or fall below the human level and become a beast." This is one of many ways of saying that nothing is what it seems to be.

9

The Eyes of Romance.

We are all apt to look at life through the eyes
of romance. This tendency to the romantic spirit
makes us get great historical figures out of perspective, sometimes to their advantage, and sometimes to their disadvantage. "Every brave life
out of the past does not appear to us so brave
as it really was," it has been said. Similarly,
many a brave life goes unrecognized. Poverty,
sickness, bitter disappointment, serious failure—
to overcome the effects of these calls for a brave
spirit. The fight with them is cruel, as relentless
as any that has to be fought on the battlefield,
and upon occasions it is a fight that lasts for a
lifetime. Many a brave heart and mind are the
possession of people who, for reasons that satisfy
them, seek to hide the possession. The will to
live keeps alive the spirit. The working woman
who really should have 1s. when she has to make
1d. suffice will wrestle bravely with the privation
and seek to conceal it. Shaw thinks poverty the
greatest crime. Many a man and woman know
it to be a skeleton, and they strive to keep it
in the cupboard out of the sight of the rest of
the world. Here is bravery allying itself to the
strongest human instinct, the instinct to keep life
going, but it is not always expressed thus. Carlyle
was brave when, discovering that one of the
manuscripts of his books had been burnt, he was

confronted with the task of rewriting it. Captain Oates was superlatively brave when he walked out of the tent of his colleagues in order that they should have a better chance of life.

Chances in Life.

Another way of looking at bravery is to think of a brave case of self-discipline. "Not to attempt a gallant deed for which one has the impulse may be braver than the doing of it." Many have natural aptitude and acquired abilities that not only create many golden opportunities for them, but also make great dangers most attractive. To seize the opportunities is right; to see through the attractiveness and to avoid the great dangers is also right, but exceedingly difficult. Life demands of each of us the application of the principle of selection. We do not realize all the chances that come our way. Similarly, we cannot truthfully say that chances to demonstrate the highest of which we are capable do not present themselves to us. "We all, or nearly all, get a fair number of chances in life," said the late Viscount Haldane, "but we often do not know enough to be able to take them, and we still may even pass them by, unconscious that they exist. Get knowledge and get courage, and when you have come to a deliberate decision, then go ahead with grim and unshakable resolution to persist. It is not every one who can do this, but every one can improve his quality in this respect. It is partly a matter of temperament, but it is also largely a matter of acquired habit of mind and object. You can train yourself to increased intellectual and material energy as you train yourself for physical efficiency in the playing field. Both means of training turn largely on self-discipline, abstention, and concentration of purpose, following on an acquired realization of exactly what it is that you have set yourself to accomplish."

We need to be judicious selectors, and from time to time we must deal with circumstances that arise out of external impositions. The measure of the success that we extract from life in terms of happiness and individual achievement is related to the persistence with which, in small as well as in great things, in trials of the mind as well as of the body, we can demonstrate bravery, and be it remembered that there are few whose bravery is called forth in responding to "the quick, sharp call."

CHARITY

"CHARITY begins at home" is one of those half
truths that must be kept in true perspective if
it is not to mislead. It is the retort bitter when
one thinks of charity that is misplaced. Why
should friends and acquaintances receive material
or spiritual considerations that are denied to blood
relations? Charity in an ideal world would be no
respecter of persons. The more deserving the case,
the more spontaneous should be charitable action.
"Our charity indeed should be universal, and extend to all mankind," said Thomas à Kempis. It
should be, but it is not, because we live in a severely
practical world, and being imperfect we cannot
maintain life on an ideal plane. There is, however,
a vast accumulation of evidence of the inherent
charity of large numbers of people.

Think of the diversity of appeals that are made
in the name of charity; of the enormous amount
of time that is spent and the energy that is
expended by voluntary workers, who cheerfully
perform tasks and shoulder responsibilities in
order that others may benefit. It may be that
the conditions that give rise to the necessity for
charity are favourable in some cases. The doors
of many hospitals are kept open because people

respond to appeals that are made in the name of charity—and humanity. Perhaps, if wielders of power and part-controllers of human destiny were more imaginative, were less earthbound, were more human, some of those doors could be permanently closed because of a lack of patients. There is nothing that cannot be judged from more than one angle.

Problems.

We extol—and rightly—the marvels of Western Civilization : how it has raised the general standard of living in the West and thrust some of its benefits into the East. Taken from another angle, it is not what it seems to be in all respects. It has created, and it continues to create, problems that we must solve. Otherwise we must perish. There are, for example, the problems that spring from man's fighting instinct. Can that instinct be eliminated or sublimated, or must humanity end civilization by universal slaughter? There are, too, health problems, physical and mental.

"All over the civilized world," states Mr. Lothrop Stoddard in *Scientific Humanism*, "the conditions of modern life seem to handicap the most intelligent elements, whose numbers are stationary or diminishing; whereas the low grade and mentally defective elements of the population are rapidly increasing. The problem of human

14

degeneration is literally a life-and-death question, involving not merely the fate of modern civilization but possibly the entire future of mankind." It also gives charity a significant place in life.

Semi-True, Semi-False.

Charity that begins and ends at home is not enough, and it is a consoling fact that there are very few people who attempt to make it enough. Rich and poor alike are not satisfied to work within the limitations that would be imposed by the literal interpretation of this semi-true, semi-false saying. Charity can be thought about in a number of ways. It is "a disposition to think well and kindly of others, and to do them good; an act prompted by this disposition; liberality to the poor, or alms-giving; alms; liberality in judging of men and their actions." People who have slums for environment and who live life on the line of existence demonstrate in their daily lives the depths of human charity, which, without reflection, instinctively, they carry into the realms of self-sacrifice. From time to time they make existence possible for their neighbours. Similarly, some "men of money," who by their acts show that they understand the right use of money, can be placed among the world's benefactors. To-day, America is looked upon as the land where huge fortunes are quickly made, and where the many

15

can attain a financial standard that is denied the inhabitants of less prosperous countries. One celebrated American millionaire, whose unostentatious giving was on a gigantic scale, at the end of his life confessed that "of all the ways of disposing of money, giving it away was the most satisfactory." (*The Secret of Success*.) Again, a Boston merchant lived his life in harmony with the spirit of a document that was found after his death. It read: "By the Grace of God, I will never be worth more than fifty thousand dollars. By the Grace of God I will give one-fourth of the net profits of my business to charitable and religious uses. If I am ever worth twenty thousand dollars I will give one-half of my net profits; and if I am ever worth thirty thousand, I will give three-fourths; and the whole after fifty thousand. So help me God, or give to a more faithful steward, and set me aside." Examples could be multiplied.

Relativity.

Some people think that the highest form of giving is the giving that deprives the giver to such an extent that the deprivation is acutely felt; that the millionaire who hands the organizing secretary of a ball for charity a thousand pounds does not act on as high a plane as the working man who gives away the pence that he needs for tobacco to his unemployed brother. Pursuit of this line of thought would involve excursions into the whole world of abstract thought and disputation about matters of feeling, to which, states Mr. I. A. Richards in *Practical Criticism*, "belongs everything about which civilized man cares most," instancing "ethics, metaphysics, morals, religion, physics, and the discussions surrounding liberty, nationality, justice, love, truth, faith, and knowledge." More pertinent to present purpose is the fact, as has been pointed out, that "There is no dearth of charity in the world in giving, but there is comparatively little exercised in thinking and speaking." A man so tender-hearted that he would go without a meal himself in order to give food to the beggar whose knock at the door he answers, can be surprisingly hardhearted when thinking about others with whom he disagrees, and reflect the hardness in caustic speech. Think of the bitterness that springs from religious bigotries, divergences of opinion on moral, ethical, and political matters, prejudices that are rooted in personal tastes, and so on. Much more charity than is often displayed by people, either educated or illiterate, in thinking and speaking, would both simplify and purify life.

Man's Limitations.

It is difficult to keep sharply defined the circles, business, private, social, in which we think it right and fitting to move. The interests, desires, and claims of others curtail our liberty. " Every listener-in has to decide everyday on some such choice as to whether he will attend to a funny man amusing a vulgar audience on a pier," states Mr. Archibald Weir, M.A., in *Others*, "or to the sort of recreation likely to appeal to the valetudinarian denizens of a health resort, or to the prayers and exhortations in some old shrine that reproduce what brought so much comfort and strength to our fathers. When he has decided, the rest are outsiders. And often there will be more significance and merit in deciding who are to be outsiders than in choosing the station that is to reach us. This is a hard saying, but as we are at present constituted it must be accepted as a bare statement of a stark fact." This is rational recognition of man's limitations, but man has progressed from the primitive to the civilized because of the expenditure of volitional force that is generated by a determination to give effect to the ideal in terms of the practical. Charity, liberality of judgment working itself out in good deeds to all men, has been a potent factor in helping forward humanity's onward march. True charity is a purifier of man, because to exercise it he must place himself in harmonious relationship with his fellow men, and such is one of the highest achievements of which man is capable.

No. 4

DETERMINATION

"THE longer I live the more I am certain that the great difference between men, between the feeble and the powerful, the great and the insignificant, is energy—invincible determination—of purpose once fixed, and then death or victory! That quality will do anything that can be done in this world, and no talents, no circumstances, no opportunities, will make a two-legged creature a man without it." These "kindly words" of Fowle Buxton strike a helpful note. They suggest that man *is* master of his fate if he has the determination to clarify his ideas on what he ought to do and on how he can best achieve his aims. But determination must be supplemented. Determination, to be basically valuable, should be an extension of clear-sightedness. It should not be one of the family of which perversity and obstinacy are members. The deliberately perverse show a measure of determination—to be perverse. The mainspring is defective and, therefore, the functioning cannot be wholly satisfactory. Similarly with the pugnacious. The fighting spirit is admirable, but the fight to justify itself must be about something that is worth while.

A World of Struggle.

Life presents us with inescapable opportunities. The world into which we are born is a world of struggle. We require suitable equipment to engage in the recurring struggles. "Up to a certain age," as has been pointed out, "a capable person delights in exerting himself or herself. After a long life these early years seem bright with little else than strenuous effort. Every avenue to exertion is welcome. If we pity our young people, it is always because the same avenues for exertion are no longer open to them. Happily, they retain the knack of finding or inventing new ones for themselves. In those years we are under the dominion of the impulses that made the earlier life of the race. Later we outgrow such primitive urgings. Exertion alone is seen to carry us not so far as we hoped. And we wake up to the influences of which we had been unconscious."

It is difficult as we pass through life to retain the spirit of youth. Youthful delight in exertion gives place to quiescent acceptance of things favourable and unfavourable. Early cultivation of the habit of maintaining a determined attitude towards performance of the tasks that periodically concern us helps throughout life.

Determination is the lubricant that keeps the wheels of progress in rotation. With the undeveloped and untrained it is often the reaction to authority. The boy or girl who at school and college determines to achieve success works under guidance and responds to stimuli. Success carries with it certain tangible prizes; it opens the doorway to chance and to privilege; it is worth while for its own sake. The young man and the young woman demonstrate belief in the spirit of determination because they must be determined in order to surmount difficulties that they cannot avoid, or because habit formation has given them a mental set that makes them prefer self-disciplined action to desultoriness.

Sincerity of Belief.

Sincerity of belief also gives rise to determination. The idealist, be his ideals right or wrong (and on such matters there are valuable lessons to be learned from understanding of the principle of relativity, not necessarily Einsteinian), sincerely believes that his ideals are worth propagating, and that for work to be concentrated on their translation from the ideal to the practical will be a wise concentration of human effort. This sincerity of belief gives vitality to determination. It need not be purely idealistic. Belief in self is the essence of self-effort, and self-effort cannot be directed and renewed without determination.

In these days of clash, many people have come to associate determination with "the hard-headed business man," who knows what he wants and is determined to get it at all costs, which his opponents think are invariably paid by his employees. Certainly, the business man of to-day needs to be determined. The business world at best is a mosaic, the variegated pattern of which needs to be well understood. Below its best it tends to create sharp contrasts, the conflicting points of which can give rise to chaos. But, really, the business man is similar to sundry other people, who, collectively, constitute modern society. He looks out on life and sees that his operations must be soundly based. He has his own set of first principles, and these he determinedly applies not only in the interests of self but also in the interests of others. Life cannot be simplified to correspond with life as it is lived in the kindergarten department. The primary of one group of adults is different from that of another, but the difference, though it often leads to competition, does not inevitably consolidate the advantage of the one to the disadvantage of the other.

First—and Fresh—Principles.

When thinking of determination as it relates itself to activities that are deliberately undertaken it is important to bear in mind the quality of first principles, and to have width, breadth, and depth of vision in order to get an intellectual conception of the consequences of the application of those principles in so far as consequences can be synthesized. The late Lord Haldane was convincing on this point. "We are bound," he stated, "to search after fresh principles if we desire to find firm foundations for a progressive practical life. It is the absence of a clear conception of principles that occasions some at least of the obscurities and perplexities that beset us in the giving of counsel and in following it. On the other hand, it is futile to delay action until reflection has cleared up all our difficulties. If we would learn to swim, we must first enter the water. We must not refuse to begin our journey until the whole of the road we may have to travel lies mapped out before us."

The search after fresh principles does not necessarily involve the searcher in inconsistencies. Truth as it may be seen to-day may be the falsity of to-morrow. Yet certain truths prevail. It is for each to find the right approach to them. "A commanding grasp of principles," wrote Viscount Morley, "is at the very root of coherency of character. 'And coherency of character is the thing that tells.' The law of things is that they who tamper with veracity, from whatever motive, are tampering with the vital forces of human progress. Our comfort and the delights of the religious imagination are no better than forms of self-indulgence when they are secured at the cost of that love of truth on which, more than on anything else, the increase of light and happiness among men must depend. We have to fight and do lifelong battle against the forces of darkness, and anything that turns the edge of reason (be it insincerity, ambiguity, or the double use of words) blunts the surest and most potent of our weapons."

Inevitability of Struggle.

This insistence on the importance of first principles, on the inevitability of clash and struggle in life, is not irrelevant to the consideration of determination. Direction goes hand in hand with determination in action. Arnold Bennett reached London with a few coppers in his pocket and became one of the world's great authors. In early days George Bernard Shaw lived on his parents and spent much time in libraries garnering knowledge, which, later, he transmutes into literary work that gains for him an international reputation. His make-up, it is true, is not "ordinary," but it is certain that it includes determination, which works itself out in accordance with the fundamental nature of the individual. A similar truth is applicable to explorers, pioneers, experimenters, captains of industry, builders of nations, and it holds good in connexion with all human beings who live life purposefully.

Determination gives point to character and potency to effort. It is one of the safety valves of emotion, and one of the methods by which thinking is crystallized. Determination affects us though it does not get beyond the realm of the abstract. Immediately it becomes active, it carries us away from or nearer to a goal. It is either for us or against us. Determination being dynamic emphasizes its quality. Thought pressed along these lines leads to the conclusion that what we determine to do and why we so determine give rise to ultimate results, realized partly by determination and partly by other factors, which are final links in the chain of life. The first links are basic principles and primary aims. Determination and other human attributes are the materials of which the whole is forged.

EFFORT

THE influence of Western civilization tends ever to create new desires rather than to intensify interest in desirelessness, which state is more expressive of life as it is lived in the East. People in the West live by competition, though modern developments make co-operation increasingly desirable, and in certain cases absolutely essential. By competitive effort most of us must live. What we get follows close upon the heels of what we do, and what we do is frequently conditioned by what must be done to make participation in the business and social life of the age in which we live both effective and pleasurable.

In the East there is desire, notwithstanding Western influences that become more and more aggressive and revolutionary in result, to seek contentment through self-denial rather than happiness through the satisfaction of ever-expanding needs. The one attitude towards life, for practical purposes, can be thought of in terms of the material and the other in terms of the spirit. Maintenance of either attitude calls for effort that arises from interest. Before life in the East can be lived on the plane of desirelessness, there must, paradoxically, be desire—the desire to dispense with non-essential material things, to harness the mind to the spiritual at the expense of the body rather than to gratify mundane requirements at the risk of effectual repression of the needs of the spirit. There must, too, be maintenance of effort not only to give practical effect to desire, but to keep effective the state of desirelessness that is brought about by translation of the ideal to the practical world of affairs.

Creative Evolution.

Think of the metaphysical principle of creative evolution, which has, thanks to the works of Bergson and others, an important place in literature that deals with theories of life. This principle is excellently stated and illustrated by Mr. Herbert W. Carr in his stimulating and compact book, *The Freewill Problem*: "The uprush and the descent of the water in a fountain are opposite directions in a movement which is one and identical. The force which brings the water down—gravitation, as we name it—is exactly counterbalanced by the force which raises it. There is an ascending and a descending movement, and if we ask which is original, only one reply is possible. The descent is consequent on the ascent. Life and matter, according to this principle, are, in the same manner, opposite directions, an ascent and a descent in a movement. Life appears as an ascending movement, as a push or impetus or spring. All the descriptive phrases which express the familiar aspect of living activity bear witness to this concept, and our experience confirms it. Expressions like 'will to live,' 'libido,' 'life-force,' and even less forceful and more usual words, such as 'effort,' 'striving,' 'endeavour,' all derive their particular intension from the idea of life as a source of energy, upward pushing, forward straining, not towards some attracting goal, but towards freedom and expansion. Against this uprush there seems a dead weight, an opposition or, rather, an obstruction. This is matter, or materialization. This materialization, at the same time that it appears as the opposite of life, also appears as the consequence of the activity of life. Every individual form of living activity grows old and finally succumbs to the materialization which puts a term to its freedom and deadens it. And what is true of the individual is true of the universal." This long quotation serves to focus attention on the place of effort in life.

Theorists and Practitioners.

Whatever theory of life we accept, we have to exert ourselves in order to function. Aims differ, and efforts that are made to give effect to them are differently valued. Metaphysicians and philosophers make oral and written pyrotechnics out of material that is provided in abundance by life's problems. They are both theorists about life's purposes and practitioners of life. Some practitioners live and leave the explanations of life to others. The ordinary man or woman in the street when faced with great difficulties that give rise to a measure of desperation demonstrates his or her attitude towards life by a terse remark such as "I must live." The cynic remarks: "I see no necessity," and the thinker is impelled to try to find a fundamental principle of life to answer the question "Why?" Further, the ordinary man or woman in insisting upon the necessity to live has also the desire to apply ways and means of living.

Attainment and Realization.

During early years conscious effort enters into the plan of life and throughout it remains part and parcel of the plan. Sometimes it requires earnest consideration because it is the precursor of activities that are deliberately undertaken to attain specific ends, and sometimes it is the instrument by which an instinct receives expression or through which adjustments are spontaneously made to ever-changing circumstances. The effort that is purposive is the effort about which it is desirable, and upon occasions necessary, to concern ourselves. Effort must be exerted to acquire knowledge so that acquired knowledge can be applied to the attainment of practical ends. Both attainment and realization may involve effort.

Self-Expression Through Effort.

Effort enters into our expression of personal desires and into our contributions as individual units of modern civilization. Both the lowly and the exalted, the rich and the poor, the normal and the abnormal, must look to effort to give practical significance to many of their ideas. Take a simple illustration. The poor must have food. If they are self-supporting they must take steps to obtain sufficient money with which to buy food. Money is one form of reward for work. The performance of work requires effort. The rich can go through life without experiencing financial worries and embarrassments. Their thoughts may turn to the attainment of power over others. To exercise power will involve effort. Or they may, in the spirit of self-sacrifice, be willing to work to advance the general good. Again, effort must be expended on giving point to the advancement of idealistic and altruistic aims. Effort, in short, is a constant companion of interest.

As individuals we become interested in causes, movements, work, recreation, and so on. Interest requires to be allied to effort to ensure development. Modern psychologists have done much to bring this fact into helpful perspective. The groundwork of education is interest and effort, which must work in effective combination. "When knowledge is new in the hands or heads of its possessors," states Professor E. T. Campagnac, M.A., in *Education*, "it affects them very much as new wealth of other kinds affects people. They are, in fact, *nouveaux riches*, they are not quite at their ease with this new thing they have acquired. They exhibit it, deliberately to make a show, or unintentionally because they cannot help it. . . . The increase of knowledge is vexatious until the new is welded and made one with the old by intelligent and habitual use . . . there are degrees of possession; there is formal possession and real possession; and real possession is not achieved until the thing possessed has become one with the possessor."

An Endless Chain.

Use implies effort. Scraps of knowledge have limited usefulness. They require to be related. To acquire scraps of knowledge needs slight effort. Indeed, the effort is often effectually disguised as pleasure. To relate the knowledge so acquired is more difficult, and more difficult still is the task of making intelligent and habitual use of knowledge. Interest forces the imagination; effort, well directed and ably applied, harnesses imagination to practical ends. Effort is exhilarating. Become enthusiastic in effort, and a danger is that it may be injudiciously pressed. Effort that is pressed causes breakdown, creates results that minimize the advantages that sound effort bestows. Only through effort can a philosophy of life be clothed in significance. To theorize demands mental effort. Theories, sometimes wrapped in the mists of idealism, are, speaking generally, of little value until effort is exerted to turn them into practice, and they are of greater value when idealistic theory has become habitual practice. No one need be lethargic through lack of opportunities to be energetic. Ambitions, necessities, pleasures, well-doing for self and for others constitute an endless chain. The more effort is exerted to weave them into the material of life the more they increase. There is no finality. The effort exerted to-day creates a new ambition that is a stimulus to renew effort. True, Dryden has it, "We ought to attempt not more than what is in the compass of our genius and according to our vein." But genius is expansive, and we are not the same day by day and year by year. This is not to deny that there is a limit to individual capacity, but to recognize one of the most inspiring and stimulating facts of life—that few of us, no matter what efforts we exert, are finally stopped by realizing that limit.

No. 6

FAITH

CURRENT opinions on faith can be helpfully sectionalized. There is one section the members of which contend that science has done much to destroy faith, and there is another section which strengthens the faithful in that the members of it are firmly convinced that, notwithstanding superficial appearances to the contrary, faith is developed by science. It matters little or nothing in the practical affairs of life which section is right or wrong. The truth, recognizable as such by all, but not similarly evaluated, is that we live by faith in many matters that we do not seek to relate to our intellectual concepts.

The greatest war in history, with its starkly realistic aspects, extended and intensified the general interest in faith. It was, indeed, faith that sent many civilians into the fighting ranks as volunteers in the early days of that "War to end War," itself, by the way, an idealistic slogan that skilfully caught up and clearly reflected the spirit of the faith of those who readily fought in order that others, as they thought, should never be called upon to fight. Faith in a Higher Power, faith in the rightness of a cause, faith in leaders,

33

faith that war is a legitimate method for human·
beings to adopt to bring about mental and spiritual
change—these were expressions of faith that were
revealed in men's actions. Afterwards came strange
disillusionment, which, however, did not kill faith.
It merely served to run faith into new channels,
and faith, faith in the ultimate attainment of
human ideals in connexion with matters military,
revived aspirations and gave hope new vitality.
Similarly, with regard to religion, science, codes
of conduct, and modes of government—faith has
from time to time rooted itself in soil that in the
end has proved to be barren, but it has planted
itself anew in virgin and fruitful soil.

Mastery of Life's Circumstances.

Faith does not die. It is one of the essentials
for the carrying on of human life. Without it,
men who are interested in strongly contrasted
human affairs would not begin and maintain
various activities that have particular and general
effects. The value of faith in life has stimulated
great thinkers to speculation. No healthy-minded
person wants to be a law unto himself or herself,
wants to live alone in supreme isolation. There
are, and there must be, sundry contacts with other
persons from whom there cannot be complete and
lasting escape. "There is no doubt," says Dr.
Horace Carncross, M.D., in *The Escape from the*

Primitive, "that much of the convention, custom, elaborate establishment, and business of our civilization is absurd, but all are agreed that a certain modicum of these things is necessary to any civilization and to the maintaining of individual decency, although there may be little agreement as to what that modicum is. As a matter of fact, we live in the particular society and age in which we are born, and squirm as we will, we cannot escape the life of that society or period. We may prefer the Periclean Age or the eighteenth century, but we are in the twentieth century and our preferences, if they make us whine, are worse than useless. Clothes, food, houses, births, laws, education, customs, health, sickness, entertainment, position, and even death itself must be reckoned with. There is no real or complete escape. The attempt to make a complete escape leads only to greater trouble, as every wise man knows. Our hope and effort therefore is to master without being swamped all these circumstances of our lives." Effort is stimulated and mastery is helped by acts of faith.

Knowing and Learning.

In an age that is rich in the successes and failures of materialism it is, perhaps, natural and inevitable that attempts should be made to stress the importance of reasoning by belittling the importance of faith. It is obvious that we must think before we act in many ways. If we would use, to satisfaction, a complicated piece of machinery we must know something of the principles on which it works, and learn how to make it work in accordance with those principles. Both knowing and learning involve thought. It is not so obvious that it is impossible for man to dispense with faith because faith is more subtle, more elusive, more indeterminate, more incapable of being tested on the anvil of practice. The scientist himself is an example of the value of faith working in man as a driving force in life. "What is the purpose of life?" asks the philosopher. The scientist in his laboratory shortens the question. "What is life?" he asks himself. Various replies are made, but the complete reply has yet to be formulated. The scientist, drawing upon highly specialized and technical knowledge, has spent, and is spending, much thought and time on scientific attempts to create life. He uses his brain, makes full use of valuable scientific knowledge, and has faith, but no guarantee, that ultimately the laboratory will divulge the secret of life. His faith in the ultimate realization of that mystery of mysteries induces him to sacrifice himself on the altar of empirical knowledge. He earnestly believes in the desirability of the testing of theory in practice. He values highly the pursuit of knowledge—and often pursues it through faith in intangible things. It is true, of course, that the implications of adherence to faith and of actions that are the outcome of faith rather than of reasoning give rise to controversy. Can faith be justified by reason? Is faith the friend or foe of the thinker? Does faith stultify thought? Is an act of faith as easily justified as an act of reason? Is not a reasoned act itself justification, and an act of faith justified only by the quality of its results? These are typical of the starting points of discussions on faith and life. Think of it from another angle.

Ancients and Moderns.

Science, it is sometimes said, is not reconcilable with religion. The advance of science, it is thought, must adversely affect religion, which owes much to faith. Much can be admitted without abandonment of the conviction that faith is essential to life. Sir Bampfylde Fuller, in *Causes and Consequences*, devotes a chapter to consideration of "Ancients and Moderns," and stresses, with other subjects, a "characteristic of the ancients—the greater insistency on their faith." He proceeds: "In those days religious beliefs were as naive as those of the nursery. Deities differed from mortals only in being stronger, more passionate, and in living for ever. There was no elaboration of creeds or subtlety of dogma:

indeed, current opinions as to the nature and attributes of particular deities were constantly changing. Beliefs showed the curious mixture of the grotesque and the sublime which so often surprises us in the religious notions of children. The future, it was held, could be divined more accurately through oracles and omens than by reasoning from the past. State affairs were guided by fortune-tellers. What should we think of our Government if, being uncertain, say, as to its Irish policy, it deputed the Secretary of State to consult a clairvoyant who lived in a grotto under the cliffs of Matlock? In ancient days nothing would have seemed more obviously appropriate; the oracle was the statesman's recognized adviser, and States vied with one another in decorating its official abode. A general would not join battle until an animal had been slaughtered and cut open, and he was satisfied that its entrails were in good condition and normally placed. Had we not freed ourselves from this superstition, Lord Haig would have insisted upon inspecting the liver of a goat, or a fowl, before issuing his orders for the day."

Disillusionment.

"These imaginings are not, of course, dead. Fortune-telling is still a profitable business; there are multitudes who think it unlucky to spill salt, to sit down thirteen to table, or to start travelling on Friday. But superstitions are dying, and it is not sacrilegious to smile at them. We have become disillusioned. To awake in disillusionment is one of man's severest trials. But he owes his sagacity to this discipline. The errors of divination have been remembered and laid to heart. Man has the capacity of reasoning from the past to the future, and has slowly extended it as faith has disappointed him. He puts more and more trust in 'common sense'." This and much other evidence of the decline of faith can be accepted *in toto* or with qualification and, at the same time, there need not be denial of the present vitality of faith.

"Creatures of Faith."

Take down from the library shelf a history that covers centuries, and its records of some of the greatest spiritual forces that have ever operated in the world will include the names of "creatures of faith," such names, for example, as Latimer and Ridley, Anne Askew and Mary Dyer, but, as the derided Smiles contends, "Time brings about strange revenges. The prosecutors and the prosecuted often change places; it is the latter who are great—the former who are infamous." Time, too, brings about changes in form rather than in spirit.

Faith, in the West, has kept alive the spirit of a religion founded nearly two thousand years ago. It has, too, led to indiscretions, and its followers have retarded rather than advanced the cause that gives it life. Even so, these "lapses" are but the results of human imperfections. Faith can easily lead to excesses. Such are the weaknesses of its inherent strength, though excess is not always bad in personal effect. The faith that gives to man relief in sorrow, the strength to resist temptation, patience in endurance, the determination to overcome adversity, comfort in disappointment, the capacity to use life to attain idealistic aims, is faith that persists. We have been told by master minds that faith is necessary to right conduct. "They are right in essence," comments Mr. William McDougall in *Character and the Conduct of Life*, "if by 'faith' we mean, not acceptance of any system of beliefs, but only the feeling that the difference between higher and lower ways of living is vastly important and that it is worth while to strive to follow the higher way according to such light as we can find. That is the essence of faith; and it remains a matter of faith rather than of knowledge: for it is something that cannot be demonstrated by any process of observation or reasoning. It is impossible to prove that, in general and from the point of view of each individual, honesty is the best policy.

And probably it is better for the moral development of mankind that no such demonstration is possible." Quite so! Faith is one of the mainstays of people who think, in all sincerity, that their acts of faith are the highest acts of which they are capable. Time sometimes proves them to be right and sometimes to be wrong. They themselves acting in good faith cannot act better, for though applied reasoning may reach the same point as faith reaches, there are occasions upon which faith transcends reasoning.

GENEROSITY

MODERN psychologists and their popular propagation of principles have helped to focus general attention on the value of the association of ideas in various processes that relate to human conduct and activities. Many of us exploit that value without being keenly aware of its full significance. Think of, or even hear, the word "Safety," and more or less automatically the mind associates with it another word—"First." This is because the enormous increase in road transport, in both urban and rural areas, has made it desirable in the public interest to educate the community, old and young, in matters pertaining to public safety. It is no longer possible to cross the streets of cities and towns in leisurely fashion. Caution must be exercised to make reasonably sure of safety—hence the injunctive slogan "Safety First." This, emphasized and reiterated in numerous ways, has certainly led to the ready linking up of "First" whenever the word "Safety" is heard. Something similar, of course, operated long before modern psychologists and their supporters, also their detractors, popularized aspects of psychology.

Instantaneous Association.

After the War mentally and emotionally disturbed people sought—some continue to seek—the aid of psycho-analysts to reveal the significance of complexes, and in the process, whatever else resulted, they learned at first hand much about the principle of instantaneous association. Adverse critics gave point to the application of this principle, variously termed by psychologists, by deriding the practice of discovering that a client hearing the word "hurly" at once thought of the word "burly"! Nevertheless, association of ideas has value. It is mentioned here to serve as preamble to consideration of generosity, which, probably in the vast majority of cases, instantly gives rise to thoughts about the ready gifts of money. Use of the word "generosity" serves to convey the idea of the free use of money, but so narrowly to restrict definition robs generosity of much of its power and beauty.

Generosity is derived from *generosus*, a Latin word, the definition of which is "a gentleman." Reflection upon the genesis and implication of generosity when the right word is borne in mind opens up many avenues of speculation and of fact. That the generous man is not a miser is a fact trite and true. He does not hoard money, but if generosity merely meant the ready and undiscriminating—or wisely selective—giving of "counters of exchange" there would be little to commend and much to condemn. Generosity with this narrow expression would give rise to ills, misfortunes, and even disasters. This has been proved by the histories of many families, and it continues to be demonstrated.

Wealth and Character.

To be financially generous may stultify the healthy development of character. Think of the father, well endowed with wealth, who is generous with his money at the wrong time in the wrong way. It is natural for him to want to do the best he can for his son. His basic nature may impel him to generosity of heart and of mind—and of action that takes the form of the provision of abundant financial means, which placed in the absolute control of the son who knows not how to use money wisely may cancel out, when it is ill used, the good that would otherwise spring from the father's generosity. Too much money can be more disastrous to the development of young life than too little.

Advancement through self-effort is very much better than the weakening of effort through lack of necessity to make it. Much depends upon the qualities of the character of the recipient, but it is obvious that demonstrators of injudicious financial generosity can easily stifle the inherent good effects of generosity of heart and mind, can, indeed, nullify the practicality of the effects before they have had full opportunities to mature. Sufficient, this, for generosity thus narrowly conceived and interpreted in human action.

Generosity means far more than the passing of money from rich to poor, as socialists and others who are interested in class conflict, social contrasts, and monetary injustices, contend. They aver, indeed, that for the rich to give to the poor can, fundamentally, be the negation of the spirit of generosity. If a millionaire voluntarily hands over, for the sake of appearances, an appreciable fraction of his vast capital accumulation to a deserving cause when that cause is in real need of much more freedom than is permitted, his voluntary gift is not expressive of generosity to the degree that is represented by "the widow's mite," the gift of which involves real personal sacrifice. But that by the way.

Birth and Breeding.

Generosus means "a gentleman" and "a gentleman," states the dictionary, is "one of good birth and breeding." Here again definition needs expansion or elaboration. "Good birth" in "the good old days" was more impressive than it is in these days of democracy. Then, it too often meant people who were born into a station of life

45

that bestowed privileges. The people of "good birth" were the people who through financial and social power "cribbed, cabined, and confined" the activities of "the lowly." They were not, as the inevitable consequence of their "good breeding," superior morally, ethically, physically, or mentally. Scientists have supplied a corrective to this viewpoint (not altogether unwarranted and yet not wholly true). "Good birth" may or may not be the gift of heredity. If it is, so much the better if the breeding is also in harmony with the birth. On the other hand, if the quality of the birth is such that scientific modification on the lines of right development is highly desirable, environmental influences, scientists have convincingly demonstrated, are potent. In them some of the strongest hopes of which human beings are capable can confidently be placed. "Good breeding" is thus not the natural and exclusive perquisite of the very few, who by fortuitous circumstances are, as it were, destined to control the many who are less fortunately circumstanced. It is conditioned in many ways by the facts of life that are created by others and also by the manner in which the individual uses those facts. "Good birth" has thus, through environment, persisting counter influences, which may, of course, accentuate the advantages of good breeding or counteract or even eliminate them.

Breadth of Conception.

More helpful conceptions of "a gentleman" can be found in the writings of famous thinkers than between the boards of any dictionaries. Turn, for example, to a work such as *Plain Living and High Thinking*, in which an idealist's theories of life and of living are fortified by the sayings of the great. "Only a refined mind," it is affirmed by the author, "is capable of generosity; of the generosity that thinketh no evil, the generosity that defends the feeble and oppressed, the generosity that dismisses unheard the anonymous scandal, the generosity that puts the best construction upon words and deeds, the generosity that never imputes motives, the generosity that never fosters suspicions. When Thackeray says that 'a gentleman is a rarer man than some of us think for,' it is because he knows how rare a quality this noble generosity is. 'What is it,' he asks, 'to be a gentleman? It is to be honest, to be gentle, to be generous, to be brave, to be wise and, possessing all these qualities, to exercise them in the most graceful outward manner.'" When conceptions of generosity are broadened out in harmony with the spirit of this quotation, it becomes clear that generosity is not an attribute as much in evidence in everyday life as some of the baser attributes of man. To attain to such a standard of conduct and to reflect

47

it day by day is to go far in the direction of the ideal.

Clash of Characters.

When we are in conflict with another it is often extremely difficult to act in accordance with generosity "that puts the best construction upon words and deeds." How difficult it is to keep suspicion in subjection, especially when we know something about the baser qualities of the person suspected. And yet it is common for any individual to admire a generous act, more particularly when the generosity is totally unexpected. The dramatist gets some of his best effects in his clash of characters: one character acts generously towards others when expectation is that the opposite of generosity will be revealed—think of the works of some of the humanists such as Galsworthy.

The War, it was said in 1914, was a war to establish in modern civilization the principle of self-determination by the application of which the peoples of small nations were to be allowed to govern themselves without reference to the special interests of larger nations. It was, in short, a blow struck in defence of "the oppressed," and as such it was generosity in action on the grand scale. Responding to "the call," many volunteers showed themselves to be idealists—an unalterable fact, though disillusionment and obliterating

48

explanations followed. Similarly, there are eminent thinkers as well as "impractical idealists," who think that war on an even more devastating scale than the Great War can be averted only by a supremely generous gesture in the right direction, which, interpreted in terms of practicality, means abolition of armaments agreed to and carried into effect by a great power.

Impersonal Generosity.

These considerations tend to crystallize thought on what may be called "impersonal generosity," which, however, is but the focused point of the generosity that is accepted and lived by individuals. It is for each individual to cultivate generosity if he or she desires to make repeated and valuable contributions to contemporary life not only in the general interests of that life, but also of the life of succeeding generations. With the overweight of materialism that has to be carried by many people in these days of machinery it becomes ever more imperative to give generosity on the grand scale full scope. Accentuation to-day tends to be on economic justice, which, incidentally, can be realized only through the generosity of those who are in a position to concede it. This fact, when present circumstances are recalled, makes it difficult to accept Junius: "How much easier it is to be generous than just."

49

It is much easier, thinking of the many implications of generosity when it is kept in full play, to agree with Pope: "Many men have been capable of doing a wise thing, more a mean thing, but very few a generous thing." Yet, generous things are done every day and voluntarily by individuals, and modern legislation certainly stresses the fact that the impersonal state is much more generous to its citizens than was often the case in "the good old days."

HAPPINESS

HAPPINESS is a state of which each individual in the course of normal life, though it falls far short of the allotted three score years and ten, has personal experience. He (and she) knows what it is to be glad or cheerful or felicitous, which words are pressed into service when attempts are made satisfactorily to define happiness. This, paradoxically, is both satisfactory and unsatisfactory. It is satisfactory in that there is an underlying guarantee in the hands of the parents at the birth of their offspring that the new life, irrespective of the circumstances into which it is born, will have a measure of happiness. It may experience many hardships in fighting the battle of life; it may be below par in health, physical and mental; it may be guilty of many actions that result in misery—but it is certain that happiness will, intermittently, break through; that, however black the clouds may be that seem to hang perpetually overhead, some of them will, true to proverb, have silver linings. So far it is satisfactory that happiness is not the exclusive possession of any one class or peculiar to human beings who can be said to have reached a specific stage in human development in its three aspects, physical, mental, and spiritual. It is unsatisfactory in that there are artificial, false, and harmful stimuli to happiness, so that happiness itself, when experienced, is of a spurious quality, though it is straining a point to deny that it is happiness when judged from the standards of the individual.

Elusive Happiness.

Happiness, though so common, is yet elusive. Though all of us know what it is, none of us can feel secure in it. Life's circumstances create happiness for us, and they quickly dispel it. There are times when we feel happy and know not why, and there are times when we squander money, spend time, and deliberately pursue happiness without overtaking it. It eludes us, is a will-o'-the-wisp, and yet all the factors over which we have control are favourable, and, cold logic would demonstrate, should produce happiness. It is not surprising that the question, "What is Happiness?" is as difficult to answer as those recurring queries "What is Truth?" "What is Beauty?" "What is Goodness?" A psychologist will consider happiness and entitle his consideration "The Problem of Happiness." Thus, for example, Mr. Everett Dean Martin in *Psychology: What It Has to Teach You About Yourself and the World You Live In*, in one section of his chapter on "Man and His Emotions" uses the heading "Psychology and the Problem of Happiness." There *is* a problem.

Who are the happy people? Why are they happy? Is the absent-minded professor who shuts himself in his study to avoid frequent contact with the outer world in order that he may remain engrossed in research work, or writing, or criticism, or construction, really happy? We all know of this type of professor through novels and stage plays—characters drawn with exaggeration and yet having prototypes. This professorial concentration on the exercise of thought related to purposive action apparently bestows satisfying happiness. There is an irresistible urge to live life in this manner; a persistent disinclination to change it for any other mode of life that appeals strongly to other human beings. If the professor is really happy, his happiness is based on something. Is it physical, intellectual, spiritual? It is apparently quite different from the basis from which springs the happiness, if such it be, of people who spend lavishly on material pleasures—the people who restlessly move about from place to place, from country to country, the people whose responsibilities are comparatively light and whose power to purchase anything that they fancy in so far as goods and services are concerned is enormous. If these people are really happy, their happiness seems to have its roots in the ability always to gratify personal whims, to indulge personal tastes. This again must differ from the happiness that is derived from self-sacrifice.

Life's Paradoxes.

Social workers see suffering, distress, poverty, sickness, hardship, as inseparable parts of the lives of people who must live in slums because they have not the means to live elsewhere, and they decide to deny themselves in order that these slum dwellers may be better circumstanced than would otherwise be possible for them. Take a glimpse at the lives of these slum dwellers, and happiness seems to present itself in an entirely different way. Social workers have a conception of happiness that urges them to work so that others may be given opportunities to introduce into their lives facts and factors that make for happiness. But, in another way, from the angle from which life is viewed slum dwellers themselves appear to be able to create happiness for themselves. They are carefree, and the happiness that they extract from widely maintained activities is more exuberant than that realized and reflected by people whose individual expressions are stultified and repressed by the rules of social and other conventions.

"The Joyous Overplus."

Happiness is manifest everywhere; the sources from which it springs are countless. Since I read

Ernest Raymond's *Through Literature to Life*,
which generates the spirit of joy in living by bringing common minds into contact with the products
of the minds of great creative literary artists, I
have often recalled what he writes about "The
Joyous Overplus." It seems to supply a key to
happiness. "In all living things," he writes, "there
is a boundless excess of life over the needs of living:
that is the fundamental fact. And this ebullient
excess, in trees and hedgerows, bursts into flower;
in larks and nightingales into a cataract of song;
in children into romping and shrieking and laughter, or into the most wonderful day-dreams and
the vividest make-believe; in adolescent youths
into ragging and rough-housing, or into towering
ambitions and splendid egotisms; in men and
women into hobbies, into enterprises, into voyag-
ings, into research, into art, into sport, into danc-
ing, into good works, into long, long talks, and
into long impossible dreams. And though in a few
men it would seem to be totally perverted, and
though in all of us it is occasionally misused, yet
a thousand times more often than not it is bearing us on the waves of happiness so soothing
and serene that we mark them no more than we
mark the hours they fill, and thus in the last
audit of our lives we credit them with immeasur-
ably less than their due." Mr. Raymond con-
siders the animal kingdom and works up to the

human: "The creation of happiness is, I think, related to the judicious use of the boundless excess of life over the needs of living."

Varying Viewpoints.

Nevertheless, the problem remains. There are men who deliberately drink themselves into a state of drunkenness because it is an escape and a realization. Neither is ultimately worth while, and yet the sequel to this deliberate act is the creation of a state that is sought after or discovered without seeking by people who can truly claim to be happy. Mr. Martin contends that "consideration of the whole problem of emotion leads us to the view that emotional balance comes very near being a psychological definition of happiness." To accept this contention, however, does not greatly help. Bentham and John Stuart Mill were of the opinion that the promotion of the greatest happiness of the greatest number should occupy Society and be regarded as the duty of the individual. Aristotle was an advocate of the doctrine of the Mean. There are some, as the modern philosopher, Mr. C. E. M. Joad, has pointed out, who have held that happiness is chiefly to be found in doing what our ancestors have done, from time immemorial. "Pray a little, hunt a little, fight a little, dig a little in the earth, and sing together in chorus, make love and go on the sea in ships, be sometimes alone with another and never too far from her," and Shaw, preacher and propagandist of the Life Force, believes that "the true joy in life" is in "being used for a purpose recognized by yourself as a mighty one; the being thoroughly worn out before you are thrown on the scrap heap."

The Art of Living.

Opinions "for" and "against" most of those expressed by the great can be cited as evidence of the "great thinking" of others. The point of contact that gives the semblance of general agreement is that happiness, like Heaven (according to some) is within. The subject has to adopt varying attitudes towards the circumstances of the objective world. It may be that there is no royal road to happiness that can be trodden by all. The royal road for one is the impenetrable jungle for another. "Emotional impulse" no doubt plays its part, but neither it nor happiness will be precisely the same in any two individuals. When considering ethics we ask, "What, at bottom, are the judgments that we usually call moral judgments? Are they merely attempts to express in words a particular kind of feeling or emotion, or are they a specific kind of intellectual judgment? Or are they neither one nor the other—neither feeling nor thought nor any combination of the

two, but something absolutely *sui generis*?"
(Rev. Hastings Rashdall, D.Litt.). Attempts to
define happiness and to discover first principles
for its realization inevitably raise similar provoca-
tive questions. Schopenhauer glimpsed basic truth
when he contended that what a man is contributes
much more to his happiness than what he has or
how others regard him. What he is is largely, if
not wholly, of his own making. Therefore, he
must master or find the secret of happiness in the
manner in which he exercises the art of living.

IMAGINATION

THE strength of Imagination can be inferred from the contention of one of the most controversial of modern psychological controversialists Coué, who averred that in the conflict between Will and Imagination the imagination always wins.

What is imagination? To reply, "The forms of mental images" does not take us far, although it is basically true. Professor H. Read, in *Reason and Romanticism*, furnishes an elaboration: "True imagination is a kind of logic; it is the capacity to deduce from the nature of an experienced reality, the nature of other unexperienced realities. And upon the depth and totality of the original experience will depend the reach and validity of the imaginative process. And if the process is kept to a quasi-logical rigidity, it may be observed that merely one kind of experience, sufficiently realized, will suffice for an almost unlimited progression of imaginative analogies: the one experience will be ballast enough to carry the author through any fictive evocation of feelings and actions."

I quote this abstruse passage deliberately. It is indicative of the pathways of thought that have to be trodden when solid foundations are sought. In simpler language imagination is the capacity inherent in each of us to proceed from the known to the unknown, not necessarily in the same direction or with the same effect.

"Imagination," we note in *Our Minds and Our Motives*, "takes various forms, according to the individual's experiences and habits—from embellishment by the liar to simplification by the thinker (e.g. the poet's terse diction, the sculptor's elimination of details, the dramatist's symbolical settings)." Here we get a clue not only to the value of imagination, but also to the ways in which it can be cultivated.

Attack through Criticism.

The imaginative sculptor eliminates detail. Epstein symbolized his conception of Day and Night in his work for the new London Underground Railway Headquarters. Many times during the past quarter of a century he has been the subject of aggressive attack through criticism. Neither his purposes nor his works have been understood, though it is probable that the figures on the B.M.A. building in the Strand, the Oscar Wilde memorial, the Venus, the Cherub, the Rima, and possibly Genesis, have a larger number of admirers than they had when they were first done. Epstein, of course, moulds material so that it becomes the embodiment of a concept that is rooted in imagination. George Bernard Shaw in 1921 wrote *Heartbreak House* which he termed a "Fantasia in the Russian Manner on English Themes." It was, in fact, symbolism cast in dramatic form, so deeply symbolical that even the dramatic critics were given "a second chance" to make up their minds about its qualities and its significance. Russian literature generally is steeped in symbolism, and is, in consequence, highly imaginative. The poet's terse diction is also richly imaginative. Shakespeare's sonnets in their expression are, paradoxically, far removed from dry-as-dust fact and yet in essence they are the quintessence of fact. This is on a par with the contention, seriously advanced, that the idealist is the realist.

Idealism and Imagination

Idealism springs from imagination. It is the sequel to the ability to see beyond the world of the actual into the world of the possible—if certain things are allowed or are made to operate. Huxley's "He who does not go beyond facts will seldom get as far as the facts" is a statement that indirectly stresses the importance of imagination. Healthy-minded people will not desire to embellish truth so that it becomes falsehood, but the power to embellish is imagination latent. The ways in which imagination works itself out in life suggest how it can be cultivated. Reading is obviously one method by which the imagination can be stimulated. Mr. A. G. Tracey, B.Sc., in *The Appreciation of Literature*, states that the best way to strengthen the powers of our minds is by the constant study of those writers whose works are distinguished for their imaginative qualities. He readily affirms that, "Few people, if asked what kind of reading would be useful for this purpose, would reply 'History'—yet some of the finest writing in our language has been put into historical subjects." He proceeds: "History, however imaginatively treated, must conform ultimately to the basic facts, and many may prefer for their reading works in which the groundwork also is the product of the imagination, and in which it has free rein over the widest fields, not having to confine itself to given details about persons, places, and things, but being able to invent for itself, and bend to its own purposes, all the circumstances that it needs. The English language abounds in such imaginative works both in poetry and prose, in essay, in novel, and in short story."

Scott and Stevenson, imaginative writers of a former generation, have their counterparts in, say, Wells and Galsworthy of to-day. But reading is not sufficient to enable the individual effectually to make all the requisite additions to "experiences and habits," to provide the raw material from which imagination is woven. Reading is a personal pursuit that imposes conditions of isolation. There is a kind of second-hand reading that is done by attendance at public play readings and in a sense at lectures, debates, discussions, etc., also the kind that constitutes the collective efforts of class students, but the reading that "makes a full man" has very largely to be done alone. Further, the habit of systematic reading is one of many desirable habits to acquire.

Broad Foundation Essential.

Imagination requires a broad foundation; it is, in fact, life itself that gives rise to various "experiences and habits." "Experience," again to quote Professor Read, "may be individual or collective, and what happens individually must also happen collectively, and thus instincts and experiences incidental to the struggle for adaptation and existence leave their traces on the mind when and in so far as it functions collectively. The aggregation of innumerable traces ensures steady response to environment."

There can be no "rising above" environment as is so commonly held. Environment can be changed, and it is changed in accordance with changing moods and circumstances. Imagination is perhaps nearer "absolute freedom" than is anything else. It can exist without learning, without taste, without truth, without purpose. It can be more sensitive than the head and more truthful than actuality. Imagination can make or mar. When the creative artist produces an imaginative work of genius it is at once seen that imagination can add great value to mental gifts, and when, as it does, imagination debases it proves itself to be the strongest of man's powers.

An Aid to Understanding.

Imagination is an aid to understanding. We require to exercise the imaginative faculty in the ordering of our own lives. In our association with others we are much more likely to understand them if we can imaginatively evaluate the significance of their lives, the motives that actuate them, the circumstances in which they work, the forces that sustain them. We begin to acquire habits from the day of our birth. We build experience into experience throughout life. Neither habits nor experiences can be kept static. There are occasions when they need to be coloured by imagination. Imagination fettered is imagination diluted, and yet it requires to be kept true to its own inherent quality, though at the same time, the world of imagination must ever be the world itself. It can be cultivated, though without cultivation it may bestow gifts that are more precious than any of the intellects. It is one of those incalculable forces in life that imposes itself upon

us and carries us beyond ourselves. It is the key
that opens the door upon other worlds, but as
its various forms are conditioned by our own experiences and habits we are compelled to recognize
when facing the facts of life that one of our primary duties in this world is so to live that our
influences, direct and indirect, make for advancement. In fulfilling that duty we beneficially exercise influence on the imaginative faculty, though
sometimes we may be tempted to think that
imagination is a heaven-sent gift that cannot
satisfactorily be cultivated by man.

JEALOUSY

JEALOUSY, it has been said, never leaves a man but with his life. Be this as it may, jealousy, "suspicious fear or vigilance," has aroused and continues to give rise to sharp conflicts of opinion among authorities who are specially interested in human life. There are some who contend that without jealousy there can be no depth of genuine human feeling. Thinkers who are pupils of this particular school of thought base their contention on observation and experience of the two sexes related in the closest bonds of intimacy. Without jealousy, they say, in effect, there cannot be true love. In opposition are the thinkers who see jealousy as "anxious carefulness," for such is one definition of jealousy. The truth as it finds expression in everyday life supports both sides, and is a constant reminder of that commonplace but highly important fact that most things in life furnish the material for the formation of more than one perfectly sound opinion.

When Shakespeare writes an immortal work such as *Othello*, taking jealousy for his basic theme, and heightens the significance of the evil of jealousy uncontrolled, he casts in the form of fiction inescapable fact of which we all need to take heed. If jealousy is "a passion which seeks with zeal what yields only misery," it were better to curb zeal in order to avoid misery. But the issue can be more readily stated than simplified. William McDougall in *Character and the Conduct of Life* writes in defence of jealousy and endeavours, not altogether convincingly, to state its proper role. He also quotes Amiel whom he avers "exhibits the fallacious way of thinking in which the common error and confusion are founded." Here is the passage: "La jealousie est une terrible chose; elle ressemble à l'amour, seulement c'est tout le contraire; elle ne veut pas le bien de l'objet aimé, mais elle veut sa dépendance à lui et son triomphe à elle. L'amour est l'oubli du moi; la jealousie est la forme la plus passionnée de l'égoisme, l'exhaltation du moi despote, exigeant, vaniteux, qui ne peut s'oublier et se subordonner. Le contraste est parfait."

Differences.

McDougall's own opinion is clearly stated: "There is a pathological jealousy which commonly is rooted in a guilty complex, a more or less repressed tendency to unfaithfulness, either actual or imagined only, or a more or less repressed memory of such unfaithfulness. And there is also an excessive jealousy which is merely a form of irritable weakness and lack of independence and self-confidence; this is apt to be shown where one partner is painfully aware of inferiority to the other in important respects, especially in respect of charm, tact, and social ease and attractiveness, in all that goes to make popularity. Putting aside such morbid and quasi-morbid instances of jealousy, which may be very distressing to both parties, jealousy has an important role to play in the lives of well-matched couples. Jealousy is the grand preservative of family life and marital faithfulness. . . . Jealousy in respect of the loved partner is, then, not only inevitable, it is also right; and it is the height of folly for young married people to pretend that they are incapable of it, or to disguise it from one another, if occasion for it arises. Every person who loves another of the opposite sex in a normal healthy way, and whose love has been accepted by that other, becomes jealous at the least sign of undue interest in, of any sex attraction experienced by that other towards, a third person. The absence of jealousy on such occasion would be sure evidence that love is absent. Jealousy is thus one of the sure evidences of love; and every one knows this so well (however violently it may be denied in the interests of some fantastic theory) that the absence of any sign of jealousy is accepted as a sign that love has departed;

and the attempt to disguise it is merely ridiculous."

Grand Preservative and Arch Destroyer.

McDougall is right when he acknowledges that his readers "will remain unconvinced." The "preservative" may be grand, but it is so rich in possibilities for evil that it would be better to discover a worthy substitute for preservation purposes. The grand preservative of marital happiness is also the arch destroyer of that same happiness. The evolution of love, under complete human control, should be built to evolve a better weapon than jealousy for the maintenance of happiness that is derived from the intimate mating of man and woman. If jealousy is, indeed, the "grand preserver," the presupposition is that this valuable weapon should be kept burnished and in constant use, for that which administers to happiness should not be sparingly used. Yet even if jealousy completely fulfils this admirable purpose, it is also one of the weapons in the armoury that can be drawn upon for many divers uses.

Look upon it as a vice or virtue, as passion or attenuated emotion, it is, as part of human make-up, available for non-marital love as well as for the important role to which McDougall refers. Often within domestic circles it is debatable whether it is not as frequently discordant as harmonious. "Jealousy, with its terrible pangs, approaching even mental derangement, is not more than the result of fear that the aesthetic union may be broken," is an opinion that runs counter to that of McDougall.

Jealousy, it is certain, is a creator of much misery. It is anticipatory in its effect. It derives its vitality from fear and functions vigorously to prevent that which never arises. It inflicts pain on self and gives pain to others. Its positive effects are bad and it succeeds in creating influences, "atmospheres," and reactions, which, basically evaluated, are much more disastrous than would be realization of the egotistic fears that give rise to jealousy and make it operative.

There are petty forms of jealousy—the sort of jealousy that springs from a nature too warm and that desires to make a relationship exclusive when restriction serves no useful purpose, and there are the forms of jealousy that are collective in influence and expression. There is a jealousy that is rooted in sharp contrasts—of rich and poor, of the free and the enslaved, of the clever and the dull, and so on.

Class Jealousy.

Can jealousy be eradicated? Hamerton, in *The Intellectual Life*, comments on existing jealousies between intellectual and industrial classes. There

is, he points out, "quite a large class of intellectual people who cannot in the nature of things
serve society effectively in their own way without
being quite outside of the industrial life." He
states a case: "We have culture because we have
paid the twenty or thirty years of labour which
are the price of culture, just as you have great
factories and estates which are the reward of your
life's patient and intelligent endeavour. Why
should there be any narrow jealousy between us,
why any contempt on the one side or the other?
Each has done his appointed work, each has
caused to fructify the talent which the Master
gave. Yet a certain jealousy *does* exist, if not
between you and me personally, at least between
our classes. The men who have culture without
wealth are jealous of the power and privileges of
those who possess money without culture; and
on the other hand, the men whose time has been
too entirely absorbed by commercial pursuits to
leave them any margin sufficient to do justice to
their intellectual powers, are often painfully sensitive to the contempt of the cultivated, and
strongly disposed, from jealousy, to undervalue
culture itself." Here, assuming the underlying
soundness of the statement (and it expresses an
aspect of truth) the pernicious effects of jealousy
have broadened out from the domestic hearth to
national life. Think of the cases of wars and

rumours of wars and realization of international repercussions of jealousy begins. Yet there is an angle from which jealousy can be glimpsed in enviable light—

> Thine own worm be not: yet such jealousy,
> As hurts not others, but may make thee better,
> Is a good spur.
>
> (GEORGE HERBERT)

It is, however, difficult, nay impossible, to strike a balance between the " assets " and " liabilities " of jealousy and definitely to state the profit or loss. If jealousy can be used to make others better without injury to self, it is well to use it. It can, but how often is it so used and how often is it used with disastrous contrary results? The correct answer gives the reply to the acid test. On the whole, it would seem better to remove it from the armoury of weapons and to wield others that are not so potentially harmful.

KINDNESS

KINDNESS is one of the expressions of self that enable us to demonstrate a fundamental belief in the oneness of human life. There can be a sort of circumscribed selfish kindness—one of the facets of egoism—which exalts self to a position of prime importance and keeps it there.

It would be stupid to blind ourselves to the fact that self requires special consideration. It is a duty that we owe to ourselves to take notice of such pertinent facts of life as eating, drinking, working, and playing. They are facts that make or mar man or woman. To indulge the palate to excess, for example, reacts upon the state of our health, which, in turn, has an adverse effect upon our mental health. To be kind to self in this sense is to eat and drink so that the physical aspects of life receive wise attention which results in the use and not the abuse of the body. So with work and play. Praiseworthy ambition may give us the urge unwisely to exert ourselves in our attempts to realize it. Excessive indulgence in play may lead to a wasting of powers that are essential for the performance of duties. But these variants of self-kindness, though important constituents of any sound scheme of self-development, spring from motives that are vastly different from those that impel us to acts that demonstrate our willingness to place others first.

To make the spirit of kindness truly operative, relationships must be established with relatives, friends, acquaintances, and even strangers. Kindness is democratic. It is no respecter of persons. All have just claims that must be met by the kind if it is within their capacity to meet them. Discriminating kindness would be farcical, a mockery, hypocritical. A hungry man is hungry whether he be friend or foe, and kindness demands that he shall be fed without a preliminary inquiry being conducted into his status. The law of the land crystallizes this idea: no one need starve if he or she is capable of getting to the type of institution, admission to which is gained by a knock and the requisite qualification—absolute poverty. And yet there must be discrimination.

Risks.

"Kindness breaks no bones" is a proverbial saying that can be counted with another common saying to the effect that upon occasions it is necessary to be cruel to be kind. The world in which cruelty masqueraded as kindness would, indeed, be a topsy-turvy world. The nomenclature, to make the saying wholly acceptable, requires special definition, although the underlying idea contains the quintessence of the spirit of kindness.

Hesitancy and Stultification.

The truly kind do not place any limit to the lengths that they will go to be kind if they themselves are convinced that what is being done is what ought to be done in the special circumstances of the moment. Upon occasions it is desirable to remember the wisdom of the wise who said: "Kindnesses misplaced are nothing but a curse and disservice," but as a generalization it is equally desirable to run the risk of doing disservice by being kind. If we do an act that we think is a kind act it is a kindness done. Disservice may or may not follow, and to arrest an act of kindness because of a problematic injury is one of those attitudes of doubting hesitancy that make for stultification. Believers in Nietzschean hardness who like to think of themselves as strong men are themselves in danger of being weak in thinking that kindness itself is evidence of weakness. They interpret too literally the rhapsodies of sentimentalists—

Little deeds of kindness, little words of love,
Make our Earth an Eden like the Heaven above.
(F. S. OSGOOD)

Yet the ultimate truth is with the sentimentalists.

75

It is difficult, taking a comprehensive view, to state an attribute that is superior to kindness. Some thinkers have not hesitated to speak of it in the superlative. Herbert, for example—

> Find out men's wants and will,
> And meet them there. All worldly joys go less
> To the one joy of doing kindnesses.

Fortunately for the advancement of man there is an abundance of human kindness that spontaneously finds expression when the need arises. It is not confined to any one class, and the motives that bring it to life are many. As man is an imperfect animal, it is not surprising that he is not always kind, and that the multiplications of kindnesses are not always thoroughly understood. Reminders of misconceptions can be remedial.

Complexity of Human Activities.

Defects must be recognized before they can be removed. "Kindness," says Smiles, the apostle of kindness, whose very enthusiasm for good doing, by word and deed, has caused him to be derided, "does not consist in gifts, but in gentleness and generosity of spirit. Men may give their money which comes from the purse, and withhold their kindness which comes from the heart. The kindness that displays itself in giving money does not amount to much, and often does quite as much harm as good; but the kindness of true

76

sympathy, of thoughtful help, is never without beneficent results." Here we get a glimpse at the complexity of human activities

Given the desire to be kind, it does not on the surface appear reasonable to think that any difficulties will arise in giving effect to desire. Thought suggestion is a helpful guide in these circumstances: "True kindness cherishes and actively promotes all reasonable instrumentalities for doing practical good in its own time; and, looking into futurity, sees the same spirit working on for the eventual elevation and happiness of the race. It is kindly dispositioned men who are the active men of the world, while the selfish and the sceptical, who have no love but for themselves, are its idlers." This, prompted by reflection upon Bentham's opinions on kindness, serves to emphasize the importance of that paradoxical necessity to learn to discriminate without discriminating. Bentham's opinions were sound. From them he deduced the principle that "a man becomes rich in his own stock of pleasures in proportion to the amount he distributes to others. His kindness will evoke kindness, and his happiness be increased by his own benevolence." His actual words were: "Kind words cost not more than unkind ones. Kind words produce kind actions, not only on the part of him to whom they are addressed, but on the part of him by whom they are employed; and this not incidentally only, but habitually, in virtue of the principle of association. . . . It may indeed happen, that the effort of beneficence may not benefit those for whom it is intended; but when wisely directed, it *must* benefit the person from whom it emanates. Good and friendly conduct may meet with an unworthy and ungrateful return; but the absence of gratitude on the part of the receiver cannot destroy the self-approbation which recompenses the giver, and we may scatter the seeds of courtesy and kindliness around us at so little expense. Some of them will inevitably fall on good ground, and grow up into benevolence in the minds of others; and all of them will bear fruit of happiness in the bosom whence they spring." If objective gain is not realized, subjective gain is assured. With benefit so obvious and so often obtained at relatively slight cost, attempts to extend the spheres of kindness cannot be too strongly praised.

Materialization of an Ideal.

The wealth of kindness in the world is cause for optimism, which itself should keep pessimism in check if it threatens to reveal itself because that wealth is not more extensive. "Let us try what esteem and kindness can effect," said Johnson. We continue to try with increasingly satisfactory results. Our Factory Acts, our social legislation, our international organizations, have greater well-being for basic object. They are necessarily the materialization of the ideal of national and international kindness. They catch up and reflect the spirit of the times, and the spirit is much more kindly as between human being and human being, as among groups of individuals with differing traditions, aims, and ideals. Human frailty explains why universal kindness is not consistently demonstrated; why there are lapses, of which we, in our quieter moments, are ashamed. "Kindness," points out Mr. Paul D. Hugon, in *Our Minds and Our Motives*, "requires strength of character (will power), both to dominate one's selfish impulses, and to convey to others an impression of friendship." Character building is a lifetime's occupation, and there is always room for improvement—a fact that amply explains why there is also always increasing scope for acts of kindness.

No. 12

LOVE

LOVE finds expression in every human life, and
yet it baffles adequate definition. It is the subject
of poetic rapture, of scientific analysis, of universal experience. It is the mainspring of the
finest acts of which human beings are capable,
and it is the root cause of lapses of human conduct
that make the reflective mindful of their primitive
origin. For love all is dared and lost, and because
of love man has scaled the highest heights of
human achievements. Reflect upon the loves of
some of the great lovers whom history notices—
Cleopatra, George Sand, Helen of Troy, The
Carlyles, Mary Stuart, Balzac, and Madame de
Hanska, Catherine the Great, Madame de Main-
tenon, Nelson and Lady Hamilton, and Queen
Victoria. Definitions of love abound; none wholly
satisfies, and yet many fully meet the mood of
the moment.

Love gives intensity to life. It arrests thought.
It quickens thought. Under its influence the inert
become keenly active and the energetic have their
energies curiously diverted, sometimes against
their wills, and sometimes in accordance with their
strongest desires. Love is a disturbing influence,

a moulding influence, an influence that creates, and an influence that destroys. What is it?

Evolution of Love.

There are cynics who contend that love is in essence and fact nothing more than sex attraction, and there are scientists who give support to this theory. Here a quotation touching upon aspects of this particular view must suffice. It is from J. W. T. Mason's *Creative Freedom*, which contains a chapter on the Evolution of Love. "Love," it is said, "is the culminating relationship in the evolution of the aesthetic influence of mating. Love, in woman, is the self-conscious form of expression of woman's subconscious desire to extend her aesthetic power of the spirituality of pure creativeness over man's materialism. Love in man is the self-conscious form of expression of man's subconscious desire to receive this aesthetic influence. Love, exchanged between man and woman, marks the union of the spiritual and utilitarian centers of life. Love is stronger in woman than in man because the initiative in transfusing aestheticism from woman to man rests on woman. The act of offering is woman's, though the offering being in such forms as feminine gentleness takes, to suggest the immateriality of pure creativeness, it is often regarded as a negative instead of an intensely positive activity. How far we must search to detect the beginning of the evolution of love is a matter of definition of what beginning is. The creative impetus has always had love of mates in view, in the sense of trying to evolve in that direction. Westermarck says: 'This absorbing passion for one is not confined to the human race. Hermann Muller, Brehm, and other good observers have shown that it is experienced by birds; and Darwin found it among certain domesticated mammals (*Descent of Man*, ii, 293). . . . In mankind the absorbing passion for one is found not only among civilized but also among savage men and women.' We may go further back, and in the relationship which flowers have attempted to establish between themselves and visiting insects we may see the first tentative movement of the creative impetus which has evolved as human love."

Truths and Life.

This is, no doubt, basic taken from a specific angle, but it is not comprehensive. It certainly includes a number of truths, some of the most pregnant truths that many human beings experience throughout their lives, but it just as certainly excludes truths that are no less part and parcel of the fibre of human lives. Take a general definition of love: "An affectionate devoted attachment, especially that passionate all absorbing

form of it when the object is one of the opposite
sex." The enlarging clause begins to lead into a
restrictive idea of love, but "affectionate devoted
attachment" justifies width and depth of meaning that help to explain a variety of human
relationships, anxieties, and interests. It permits,
moreover, of a linking up of the personal and
the impersonal. The attraction of opposites is
patent: perhaps ineradicable. When it becomes
virile, reason, logic, success measured by accepted
normal standards, discretion, are ignored or swept
aside. The power of love is one of the greatest
forces that have to be controlled and directed by
human beings.

Think of Shakespeare—

> But love, first learned in a lady's eyes,
> Lives not alone immured in the brain;
> But with the motion of all elements,
> Courses as swift as thought in every power;
> And gives to every power a double power,
> Above their functions and their offices.
> It adds a precious seeing to the eye;
> A lover's eyes will gaze an eagle blind;
> A lover's ear will hear the lowest sound,
> When the suspicious head of theft is stopp'd;
> Love's feeling is more soft, and sensible,
> Than are the tender horns of cockled snails;
> Love's tongue proves dainty Bacchus gross in taste:
> For valour, is not love a Hercules,
> Still climbing trees in the Hesperides?
> Subtle as sphinx, as sweet and musical,
> As bright Apollo's lute, strung with his hair:

And, when love speaks, the voice of all the gods
Makes heaven drowsy with the harmony.
Never durst poet touch a pen to write,
Until his ink were temper'd with love's sighs;
O, then his lines would ravish savage ears,
And plant in tyrants mild humility.

In practice the force generated by love is not always controllable. It creates other passions and gives them intense virility. Jealousy, on the one hand, is often hand in hand with love on the vicious side of life, and, on the other side, on which are demonstrated some of the finest virtues of human beings, love is equally as operative. There is the love of person for person, but not necessarily of the opposite sex.

The Normal and the Abnormal.

I mention, *en passant*, that abnormal types about which there is intermittent discussion create only a minor problem, though some critics exalt it to a major position.

Then there is the love of parent for offspring. Mother love reveals human attributes that are not second to any of which human beings are capable. It is love that demands self-sacrifice, devotion, constancy, sympathetic understanding, renunciation. It demands these and more from time to time, and they are given readily and without stint by parent for offspring, and in some cases even for the offspring of others. Children are "adopted" because of the irrepressibility of the urges to which loving desires give rise.

As it is difficult to escape, another expression of love must be noted—through love one generation gladly shoulders many responsibilities and makes many sacrifices in order that the next generation may be advantaged. Further, and enigmatically, even materially-minded people who think in terms of what they can prove for themselves during this life, and who do not necessarily order any of their activities because of any theories of a subsequent life or lives, are willing, through love, to deny themselves in order that others may profit. This is altruism, one ingredient of which is love.

Love of Country.

Then there is love of country. For "affectionate devoted attachment" to the Motherland or the Fatherland men brave all and die. The prevention of war is the subject of academic, political, and economic discussion; the waging of war is made possible by the persistence of the spirit of patriotism—and by other things. Patriotism persists because of the love of citizens for the particular country in which they are born and in which they grow to adulthood. Analysed with calculating rationalism, patriotism is a complex reality that blends the good and the bad. There is, however, no denying the strength of the love that it can engender. Was it not Cicero who said: "Dear are our parents, dear our children, our relatives, and our associations, but all our affections for all these are embraced in our affection for our native land"? An attachment that strikes so deeply is assuredly affectionate and devoted.

Again, think of love of work. A phrase that is part of the currency of everyday expression is evidence conveyed in simple direct form: "A labour of love" is the labour that we willingly undertake regardless of cost. We do it because we feel and think that we ought to do it or that we must do it. No thought of personal gain is in our minds. The impelling power of love is the volitional love. Here are reminders of love unfettered, that is sexless as far as any action that emanates from an individual can be without traces of sex—the sex of the individual cannot be separated entirely from the action of the individual— and that carries on life as effectually as it can be carried on, though the form is sharply contrasted with sex attraction and its ultimate consequences.

A Spiritualizing Force.

When thinking of love it is better to eschew dogmatism and to broaden outlook. Love can be one of the greatest spiritualizing forces in life, and

it can be coarsely materialistic if it is not shot
with idealism. Galsworthy in his essay "Delight"
gives thoughts on love an idealistic turn, a purify-
ing and uplifting urge when he writes of love as
of "the quality that lies in deep colour, in music,
in the wind, and the sun, and in certain great
works of art—the power to set the heart free from
every barrier, and flood it with delight."

No. 13

MODESTY

Is modesty the expression of a highly developed and sensitive personality? Is it the accompaniment of high intelligence? Is the modest person a sound judge of the desirable and the undesirable in conduct who orders life in accordance with the soundness of the judgment? Is the spirit of the twentieth century conducive to the cultivation of modesty and the reflection of it in everyday life? Has modern psychology strengthened or weakened the case for modesty? These are a few questions that can be asked when serious consideration of modesty and its effect on the development of personality is undertaken.

Modesty, according to the dictionary, is humility; purity of thought and manners: becoming behaviour; chastity, purity; moderation. It follows that the modest person is a person who is "restrained by a sense of propriety," who is "not forward," who is "decent, chaste, pure, and delicate" in "thoughts and language," who is "not excessive or extreme"; who is "moderate." Here, then, are the accepted bases of modesty.

G. B. S.

Now think of the first question and draw upon the life of George Bernard Shaw for material for one answer. Shaw has written himself into international fame. The letters "G.B.S." are all the identification mark that is wanted by large numbers of people in all parts of the world to name one who by the imposition of literary genius has impelled world-wide recognition. His genius, thus extensively recognized, is unknown to many to whom he is known by initials or name because for years modern journalism gave newspaper readers Shavian paradoxes and extravagances so frequently that he came to be known by "ordinary" people, without special interest in the making of books and plays, as a clever man with a great opinion of himself.

Shaw has never shown a rigid belief in abstention from the "excessive or extreme." Take one of his characteristic prefaces, that given in the volume entitled *Three Plays for Puritans*. One section "Diabolonian Ethics" opens thus: "There is a foolish opinion prevalent that an author should allow his works to speak for themselves, and that he who appends and prefixes explanations to them is likely to be as bad an artist as the painter cited by Cervantes, who wrote under his picture 'This is a Cock,' lest there should be any mistake about it. The pat retort to this

thoughtless comparison is that the painter invariably does so label his picture. What is a
Royal Academy catalogue but a series of statements that This is The Vale of Rest, This is The
School of Athens, This is Chill October, This is
the Prince of Wales, and so on? The reason most
dramatists do not publish their plays with prefaces
is that they cannot write them, the business of
intellectually conscious philosopher and skilled
critic being no part of the playwright's craft.
Naturally, making a virtue of their incapacity,
they either repudiate prefaces as shameful, or else,
with a modest air, request some popular critic to
supply one, as much as to say, Were I to tell
the truth about myself I must needs seem vain-
glorious: were I to tell less than the truth I should
do myself an injustice and deceive my readers.
As to the critic thus called in from the outside,
what can he do but imply that his friend's tran-
scendant ability as a dramatist is surpassed only
by his beautiful nature as a man? Now what I
say is, why should I get another man to praise
me when I can praise myself? I have no dis-
abilities to plead: produce me your best critic,
and I will criticize his head off. As to philosophy,
I taught my critics the little they know in my
Quintessence of Ibsenism; and now they turn their
guns—the guns I loaded for them—on me, and
proclaim that I write as if mankind had intellect

without will, or heart, as they call it. Ingrates:
who was it that directed your attention to the
distinction between Will and Intellect? Not
Schopenhauer, I think, but Shaw. . . . I am a
natural-born mountebank. . . . When an actress
writes her memoirs, she impresses on you in every
chapter how cruelly it tried her feelings to exhibit
her person to the public gaze; but she does not
forget to decorate the book with a dozen portraits
of herself. I really cannot respond to this demand
for mock-modesty. I am ashamed neither of my
work nor of the way it is done. I like explaining
its merits to the huge majority who don't know
good work from bad. It does them good; and it
does me good, curing me of nervousness, laziness,
and snobbishness. I write prefaces as Dryden did,
and treatises as Wagner, because I *can*; and I
would give half-a-dozen of Shakespeare's plays for
one of the prefaces he ought to have written.
I leave the delicacies of retirement to those
who are gentlemen first and literary workmen
afterwards. The cart and trumpet for me." In
another section "Better Than Shakespeare?"
he explains his play *Caesar and Cleopatra*, and
states: "It will be said that these remarks can
bear no other construction than an offer of my
Caesar to the public as an improvement on
Shakespeare's. And, in fact, that is their precise
purport."

Difficulties of Definition.

Some young folk at meetings of "modern" literary societies have not hesitated to label some of Shakespeare's work "piffle," but none has probably publicly declared himself to be competent to improve upon Shakespeare. The long Shavian extract is given because it is a convincing negative answer to the first question. Shaw is both highly developed and sensitive. He admits his inability to be mock-modest. There are many people who are repelled by what they consider is his inability to be "restrained by a sense of propriety," and who, in consequence, miss some of the pure thoughts that have been expressed in writing—in beautiful, pure English—during the past half century. Any attempt to reach agreement would probably break down with endeavours to frame universally accepted definitions of "mock modesty," "modesty," "propriety," etc., used in this connexion.

McDougall points out that conscience and sociability, play, curiosity, and acquisitiveness all begin very early in life, and that modesty, with love and other human attributes, comes later. Modesty is, of course, something that is peculiar to mankind: there is slight evidence of it among the lower animals. As it finds expression in the lives of human beings it has effect in practical affairs that are pleasurably contradictory.

Modesty, as it is generally understood, is not an attribute upon which Shaw has relied; lack of it has, indeed, helped him to increase the circle of his readers and so to achieve one of his objects—to bring heretical and unorthodox views before the notice of large numbers of people with the object of converting them to his point of view on matters economic, political, theological, etc.

When thinking of modesty, thought should be given to the repercussive effect of modesty on other people. Modesty in the modest person can be a form of both conceit and of deceit. Deliberate self-depreciation in moments of obvious triumph will strike some people as being the quintessence of charming modesty; it will strike other people, equally as intelligent, equally as capable of differentiating, in general terms, the desirable and the undesirable, as being a false and an artificial reticence. Humility, a close relative of modesty, is kept active or quiescent by consciousness of capacity. Modesty confronts others with the necessity of discovering truth at second hand, which is not always the best method of making the discovery. "Modesty has died out," it was declared by Theognis, one of the B.C. Greek writers whose morals as poet were "censured" as being "neither decorous nor chaste." The declaration may have been coloured by heavy personal bias, but if it was untrue in those dim and distant days there

are many who to-day are making asseverations
and are sincere in the belief that the generally
admitted lack of modesty that is characteristic
of certain aspects of contemporary life is preferable to the false modesty that "cribbed, cabined,
and confined" our ancestors, without bestowing
many, if any, compensatory gifts. Goethe, whose
high intelligence cannot reasonably be denied,
cited modesty as a special attribute of the low
born ("Only low born fellows are modest; men
of spirit rejoice over their feats"). Yet others
have been equally as dogmatic in an entirely
different spirit. ("No age, sex, or condition is
above or below the absolute necessity of modesty; but without it one is vastly beneath the
rank of man."—Barton.) Here modesty is placed
with the attributes that are indispensable to
manhood.

Time Brings Change.

If modesty be too narrowly defined, or if it be
ungenerously imposed, it results in harmful ex-
clusiveness. We live in days when to say more
than the facts warrant or to shout aloud untenable
statements so that all may hear are accepted as
part of normal activities, though, of course, their
normality does not necessarily either justify the
sayings and the shoutings or make them preferable
to, or better than, reticence and silence. Modesty,

like style in dress, changes with the times. Thus, confidently to lean for support against any dogmatic statements may be misplaced confidence. Think of Addison with his "true modesty avoids everything that is criminal; false modesty everything that is unfashionable." It were better to avoid the bumptious arrogance that conveniently forgets facts in order to "improve with importance" self-effacing depreciations that give rise to misleading conceptions. Modesty is "all right in its place," but it should not be permitted to leave its place at the expense of truth.

No. 14

NERVOUSNESS

"THE nerves, they are the man," was the dogmatic opinion of Cabanis. This is one of those half-truths, picturesquely expressed, about which it is unwise to dogmatize. The nervous system is highly important, and must be in healthy working order for man or woman to have reasonable chances of living a healthy life. But the brain is important, thoughts are important, ideals are important—the enumeration could proceed apace without exhausting the variable significance of half-truths if the conclusion be that brain or thoughts or ideals constitute the man. It is invariably wise to be chary of comprehensive statements. Often in taking too much for granted they do not take cognizance of other points of view, basic and therefore equally as important.

The literal anatomical definition of the nervous system mentions "the brain, the spinal cord, and nerves collectively," and for a closely reasoned, authoritative treatise on scientific lines of this highly important system it is well to consult specialist works, for there are intricacies and complexities that the lay mind can better guess at than describe with meticulous accuracy. This is the note that is firmly struck by P. G. Hamerton in opening *The Intellectual Life*. He begins: "So little is really known about the action of the nervous system, that to go into the subject from the physiological point of view would be to undertake a most difficult investigation, entirely beyond the competence of an unscientific person. . . A paper was read several years ago before the members of a society in London, in which the author maintained that mental labour was never injurious to a perfectly healthy human organization, and that the numerous cases of break-down, which are commonly attributed to excessive brain-work, are due, in reality, to the previous operation of disease. This is one of those assertions which cannot be answered in a sentence. Concentrated within the briefest expression, it comes to this, that mental labour cannot produce disease, but may aggravate the consequences of disease which already exists." It will not serve any useful purpose here to attempt to dip deeper into this aspect of the subject.

Take next, then, a dictionary definition of nervous. It is: "Having nerve: sinewy: strong; pertaining to the nerves: having the nerves easily excited or weak." It is at once seen that with whatever ease any individual can leave the scientific treatment of nervousness to the specialist, he or she cannot live without intermittent reminders of the necessity to keep the nervous system in mind. Mr. Hamerton in his references to the nervous system makes the point that all intellectual labour proceeds on a physical basis and warns his imaginary "young man," to whom the constructively helpful letters are addressed: "Difficult as it may be in some instances to ascertain quite accurately whether an overworked man had perfectly sound bodily health to begin with, obvious as it may be that in many break-downs the final failure has been accelerated by diseases independent of mental work, the facts remain, that the excessive exercise of the mental powers is injurious to bodily health. . . . No man can safely forget this, and act as if he were a pure spirit, superior to physical considerations."

Paradoxical Effects.

Even when the fact is kept well in the forefront of consciousness, it is not always easy to overcome adverse effects of nervousness or to turn the beneficial effects of nervousness into practical channels. We think of the nervous person as a person handicapped. Paradoxically, the handicap can be helpful. Nervous tension in people varies enormously. "Our temperaments differ in capacity of heat, or we boil at different degrees," said Emerson. The differences are in part attributable to the functioning of the nervous system. "Nearer the primitive, farther from nervous sensitiveness," is a generalization that does not do gross injustice to human beings. Develop the physical, and the necessity to keep mental development on the move must be faced if balance is to be maintained.

The creative artist is more sensitive to external influences than the manual labourer. His greater sensitiveness is not necessarily evidence of superiority. It is simply proof of fundamental differences. Certain types of people are given more credit than they deserve, because they merely do what it is in accordance with their fundamental nature to do. The "born" writer or painter is merely a bundle of abilities, aptitudes, and potentialities. He functions in accordance with them. His work is more interesting, perhaps more highly evaluated by modern society—but false values easily creep in. The painter would possibly be unable to do the work of certain manual workers whose work is essential to the very existence of modern society. This fact alone begins to undermine confidence in demonstrations of superiority that are too readily accepted in these democratic days. But this by the way.

Sensations and Thoughts.

Each individual is, in part, dependent upon the functioning of the nervous system, and when it is below par in quality, or when it is weakened,

or when it is too severely tested, it begins to
impinge upon life in general. Complexes follow.
"When an impression is made on a sense organ,
the sensation derived from it is telegraphed up
the connecting nerve fibre to the brain and there
translated by a process of which we know nothing,
from a sensation to a thought." In this manner,
Miss Violet M. Firth, in *Machinery of the Mind*,
describes how an idea enters the mind. She also
points out: "When an idea enters the mind it
does not remain an independent unit for very
long. It seems to be a fundamental characteristic
of ideas that they form alliances among themselves, and these groups of ideas are technically
known as COMPLEXES. A complex may be compared to the branching growth of a pond-weed;
it has a central starting-point from which ramify
threads that divide and subdivide, and branch in
every direction, and connect it with other systems
of ideas that have similar branching threads.
Thus it is that if an idea on any subject enters
our consciousness, we find that it is not an isolated
unit, but one end of a chain which branches into all
sorts of side issues; we have not touched a single
line of thought, but a whole railway system."

Causes and Consequences.

Nervousness can be the crystallization of a
complex. It is revealed by people in all walks of

life and by people of all ages. It is caused by fear, by anxiety, by intensity of desire, by keen anticipation, by thoughts of failure and of success, by the performance of tasks that are well within the range of acquired ability to perform them, and by the thought of having to attempt to do things about which doubts of capacity legitimately exist. It gives some kinds of efforts greater virility than they would otherwise possess, and it deprives efforts of vitality. In some cases it makes the normal abnormal and is helpful. A person extended by nervous tension will succeed beyond expectations, will surpass himself or herself. Sometimes the success will exact a physiological penalty. In other cases it will clog the wheels of action so that they cannot revolve with normal speed and sureness. The causes are often complex; the cure may be simple or there may be no cure. Take a simple case.

A lady has to enter a crowded public hall to take a seat in the front row. She is timid and dislikes crowds. The mere thought of having to walk the length of the hall under the gaze of many people gives rise to great nervousness, that "restless condition of the organism due to a mental conflict such as an anticipation of pain or pleasure." The cure, say the psychologists, is to steel herself to make the entry and to fortify herself by suggesting to herself all the reasons

why she should not be afraid to enter the hall
and to give great emphasis to them, thus keeping
in the background the reasons why she should
be afraid.

This kind of cure is more easily stated than
carried into practical effect. Yet remedies on these
lines can be brought about if complex factors
can be skilfully related.

Mental Healing.

"Mental healing" in connection with nervousness, it has been pointed out, must proceed thus:
"The thoughts to cover any nervousness are ones
of peace, poise, and power. There is no twitching
of the nerves; there is no strain or struggle in
the universe. Next move harmoniously, quietly
and normally, and this motion, which is the
motion of life, is the truth about the one you
are treating." The power of suggestion must be
exercised. Certainly peace, poise, and power can
be useful allies. Excessive nervousness leads into
diseased states. Any legitimate actions to avoid
it should be adopted. But that state of nervousness which calls up resources of strength and of
vigour that are needed for the accomplishment
of worthy tasks and that can be replenished
without harm having been done, can safely be
regarded as an attribute that gives rise to desirable
activities.

OBSERVATION

MANY people by the exercise of eyes and brains would succeed in getting considerably more out of life than they manage to get and without any cost or much trouble; indeed, they would be better for training the eyes to see and the brain to record intelligently the things that are seen. Observation is a habit of mind that brings the eyes into interesting and helpful action. Comparatively few people are keen observers by nature. It is natural for us to make less than the maximum use of our faculties, and common for us to train to the required stage of efficiency the faculties that we must use, or to develop the habits that we need to make life run with acceptable smoothness.

The producer of a play is a keen observer of the various details of production. He has to be quick in the detection of faults in deportment, of defects in the use of the voice; he must "have an eye" for stage pictures, must be able to see the incongruous in colour blends, and so on. The typist in the office, the professor in the laboratory, the agriculturist in the fields, the workman at the bench, the aviator in the aeroplane, the policeman on his beat, the detective following up a clue or attempting to get on the track of a criminal, the master at the wheel, the engine driver on the footplate—all these widely differing classes of people have sooner or later to become observant in the varied activities that are of special interest to them. This is applicable to all of us.

The Mind's Eye.

To be observant does not necessarily mean seeing with the eyes. There is a much more important essential, "seeing with the mind's eye," from the observed results of hearing with the ears and of feeling with the hands. The position is excellently summed up by Sir John Adams, M.A., B.Sc., LL.D.: "To cultivate observation . . . is not to train the eye, the ear, the hand, to extreme sensitiveness, but rather to work up well-organized knowledge within the mind itself. If we desire minute observation in a definite direction, we must cultivate special knowledge to correspond. If we wish to encourage general observation, we can only succeed by cultivating wide interests. . . . The reciprocal interaction of interest and knowledge in relation to external facts is what ought truly to be called observation." This goes to the root of the matter. "Seeing with the mind's eye" presupposes interest and knowledge.

Interest and Knowledge.

Edward Garnett wrote an appreciation of the naturalist, W. H. Hudson, which can usefully be quoted because of its relevance to the indispensability of "seeing with the mind's eye" in so far as observation is concerned. "Hudson's nature writing," wrote Garnett, "appealed to the mind, to the heart, and the senses together. In his intense appreciation of beauty in nature, however, he far outstrips all his fellow naturalists." Why this superiority? "His observations of bird life are unique for the intensity of sympathy and delight with which he cast himself into their world and mirrored their kingdom for us through the glasses of his passionate joy in shining loveliness." Hudson's nature writings give pointed emphasis to the basic sentence of Sir John Adams's point of view. In the absence of "interest and knowledge," Hudson's descriptive powers of expression would have been inadequate. He could not have caught and reflected the spirit of nature. He was interested, he knew, and he was fortunate in the possession of a facile and descriptive pen. The combination explains his distinction. There are nature lovers who have observed many of the facts that are so interestingly described by Hudson, but lacking the literary gift they cannot give written expression to their observations. To them, however, as nature lovers, Hudson's observation does not appear to be as remarkable as it does to people who have not a special knowledge of nature, and who require to have their interest in it stimulated by the questions and comments of others. To suggest to nature lovers the need to note the interesting things that are discoverable in field and hedgerow, or hill and dale, would be superfluous. Willy-nilly, they observe these things (1) because they have acquired special knowledge, and (2) because they are interested in making new discoveries, in noting again and again the things of nature that give them pleasure or that for any reason are worthy of note. Nature tells them something, and the more it tells them the more points of contact with nature they possess.

The Mind and New Ideas.

What is true of nature lovers is true of any who have special interests. In psychological phraseology, they build up "apperception masses." Re-study, for emphasis, Glover's *Know Your Own Mind* : "An idea presents itself for the first time to the mind, effects an entrance into consciousness, and is there acted upon. Herbart holds that the action of the mind upon this new idea is influenced —indeed practically determined—by the mass of ideas already present. This action is known by the name of *apperception*. This is so important that it might be well to give several definitions.

Steinthal tells us it is 'the union of two mental groups, in so far as it gives rise to cognition.' Professor Stout says it is 'the process by which a mental system appropriates a new element, or otherwise receives a fresh determination.' While Lange conceives it as 'that psychical activity by which individual perceptions, ideas, or idea-complexes are brought into relation with our previous intellectual and emotional life, assimilated with it, and thus raised to greater clearness, activity, and significance.' Dr. Hayward is simpler: 'Apperception,' says he, 'is the process of interpreting some new fact or experience by means of our previous knowledge,' but for brevity and simplicity combined it would be hard to beat William James, with his, 'it verily means nothing more than taking a thing into the mind.'"

Essential Relationships.

Here, then, is one acceptable solution of the problems that arise out of the cultivation of observation. It would be absurd, if not wholly futile, for any one desirous of cultivating the habit of general observation to proceed on the assumption that anything that is observed must sooner or later be of service and that therefore everything observable should be observed. This would be disservice to self. There must be relationships. Knowledge must be built upon knowledge. There must be that "seeing with the mind's eye." The non-specialist in the presence of the specialist is often made to feel the force of this fact. If an artist and a non-artist visit a picture gallery to see the latest works of Sargent, or Brangwyn, or Augustus E. John, assuming that both visitors have normal vision, the one will see the works with the eyes and understand them through the mind, understanding springing from knowledge of the theory and practice of the art. The other will merely observe the works and at best imperfectly understand them. What he knows of colour, or of proportion, or of perspective, and so on, will be linked with his facile observation, but not being an artist the knowledge essential to complete understanding will be lacking. A similar truth is applicable to an engineer and a non-engineer seeing machinery in an engineering department, and to any other type of specialist and non-specialist.

The Wise Man's Task.

A common saying, sometimes given as advice and sometimes in a spirit of criticism, "keep your eyes open" is not enough. To it must be added, "and your mind well stored." The greater the store the greater the power of observation. "Appearances to the mind are of four kinds," said Epictetus. "Things either are what they appear to be; or they neither are, nor appear to be; or they are and do not appear to be; or they are not and yet appear to be. Rightly to aim in all these cases is the wise man's task." Wisdom is not so much a matter of the acquisition of knowledge as the value of the uses that are made of knowledge that has been acquired.

All observation need not, of course, be utilitarian in aim. Observation for non-occupational purposes can give pleasure. Every time we see a landscape we do not need to attempt consciously to relate our evaluation of its aesthetic appeal to first principles. The knowledge that we possess provides us with the basis for spontaneous comparison, and as we observe the landscape we do not need to do more than enjoy without analysis what we observe. There is "pure delight" in gazing "upon the verdant fields below, Where Nature's ample reign, extending wide, Displays her graces with commanding pride" (Elizabeth Barrett Browning), especially after a hot summer's day spent in the noisy, petrol perfumed streets of London. Even so, the "pure delight" is intensified when the "gazing" automatically links itself with knowledge that can illumine and reveal.

Enriching Life.

Observation enriches many experiences of life. As an instrument of education, it makes the world a textbook. Some of the chapters are easily mastered, others are difficult, and a key may be necessary. Observation, linked with knowledge, is such a key. "To cultivate habits of wide general observation," says Glover, "you must cultivate wide general knowledge. An ignorant man does not observe widely; he gapes." All of us gape or stare or look vacantly at some time or other. We talk to a person dozens of times and cannot tell the colour of his hair. We "cannot say" or we "did not notice" upon many occasions when we are asked about the guests we have met at a party, the actors and actresses we have seen in the theatre, even the business men with whom we habitually associate. Often non-observance does not involve us in serious consequences. Once, however, become conscious of what is missed by inability to observe so that observation is significant and the values are practical, pleasurable, and educative, and there is hope that consciousness will lead to cultivation of a power the exercise of which eliminates many handicaps and disadvantages. The power to observe is within the reach of all; its strength is dependent upon circumstances that are not wholly within our complete control.

PREJUDICE

THE foundations of prejudice, an attribute of mind, are often laid during childhood. This fact, however, does not preclude possibilities of the development of prejudice in later life. Prejudice is an index of character, and what it tells of character is often adverse criticism. The prejudiced person is incapable of impartiality concerning the things that give rise to his (or her) prejudice. He is a victim of intellectual blindness. He may be a keen thinker and a sound judge of many matters, but once he permits prejudice to enter into his thoughts and actions he is no longer a reliable appraiser of values.

Perhaps the female sex, on the whole, harbours more prejudice than the male, though there are many exceptions. The explanation is that prejudice is rooted in emotion rather than in thought. The mind is given a certain "set" or bias in early days, which bias is not entirely eliminated by the exercise of thought in later life. The teaching of geography and history, for example, tends to throw up in sharp relief certain fundamental racial differences that are not seen in true perspective. One consequence is that some people get false ideas of foreigners, and, in many cases, never succeed in completely shaking off falsity.

Prejudice fights with reason and hopes to be the conqueror, but it is not always successful, otherwise the evils of early education, both at school and in the home, would remain with us throughout life. That evils, among which prejudice must be included, need not persist, though they become deeply ingrained before the stage is reached that brings vivid consciousness, is a basic fact from which hope arises.

A Serious Vice.

Lord Beaverbrook in *Success*, writes strongly on prejudice, which he contends is: "The most common and, perhaps, the most serious of vices. . . . It is," he states "a thing imbibed with one's mother's milk, fortified by all one's youthful surroundings, and only broken through, if at all, by experience of the world and a deliberate mental effort. Prejudice is, indeed, a vice in the most serious sense of the term. It is more damaging and corroding in its effects than most of the evil habits which are usually described by that term. It is destructive of judgment and devastating in its effect on the mentality because it is a symptom of narrowness of outlook on the world. The man who can learn to outlive prejudice has broken through an iron ring which binds the mind. And yet we all come into the world of affairs in early youth with that ring surrounding our temples. We have subconscious prejudices even where we have not conscious ones. Family tradition, early instruction and upbringing fasten on every man preconceptions which are hard to break."

Strength of Resistance.

This statement of fact gives an idea of the strength of resistance that must be offered to prejudice as we become conscious of it and desire to remove it. The temptation to look upon our own prejudices as helps and to think of those of other people as hindrances to self should be resisted. Each of us has sufficient work in hand (1) to acknowledge the existence of prejudice, and (2) to work systematically to remove it, without becoming purblind about the prejudices of others. Yet these prejudices are bound to impinge upon the interests and activities of any with whom their possessors come into contact.

Reformers, welfare workers, propagandists, preachers, politicians, public speakers, business men—all need to take into consideration the prejudices of others, though they themselves are probably not devoid of prejudices. Few of us are, though we differ in the manner in which we handle them.

Sense of Values.

Ford Madox Hueffer in *The Critical Attitude* gives his readers pertinent reminders of common human weaknesses, reminders that have a lesson for any who, conscious of prejudice, wish to remove it. Nothing, he states, "is more difficult, nothing is more terrible than to look things in the face." We all like to believe what we want to believe. We wish to have our own ideas accepted, our foibles applauded, and our prejudices respected. "The tendency of humanity," proceeds Mr. Hueffer, "is to give to all its settled ideas an equal value, and most men upon hearing the theory of the solar system attacked would exclaim: 'What next?' for they would foresee that by encouraging this one iconoclast, they would be opening the door to men who would desire to test and to shake all other accepted ideas. If the sun were dethronable, so also they would feel would be the British Constitution, British family life, the law of marriage, and the very laws of property themselves. . . . The fact is that a man of action feels that he cannot with assurance pursue the course marked out for him by his will if his intellect be troubled by doubts. Upon the face of it one would say that mankind, seeking as it does for novelties, would welcome new ideas, would find in them something fresh, something delightful, something interesting. But this is not the case. The fact is that new ideas almost invariably affect our sense of values—our sense of the whole values of everything."

Men cling tenaciously to old ideas and thus give free rein to prejudice. Reflect upon the results of early influences that are the outcome of education, observation, and habit.

Children of the West are taught, or they acquire in many cases, a non-humanistic conception of the coloured races. White *v.* Coloured crystallizes a definite human conflict. It also gives a feeling of superiority. It is not a flight of imagination to contend that in most cases this conception of the racial inferiority of coloured men or women when compared with white men and women is rooted in prejudice. Irrespective of the confirmation or the confutation of it by science, it is a prejudice that persists. True, it is sometimes dormant, but its very dormancy is a danger. It is latent evil that can be worked upon for evil (or good) ends.

Racial prejudice makes war possible. It is an evil of which sensitive and sensible people are ashamed in moments of lucidity, and that leads them, when thrown off their guard, to participate in activities the consequences of which they regret. But much more than prejudice must be taken into consideration in an endeavour to explode racial antagonisms. They are not sufficiently near to the lives of most people to influence normal everyday life.

Religious, social, and political prejudices are more real because they hold in them truths that few altogether escape—or want to escape. "The advantage of prejudice," again to quote Lord Beaverbrook, "is the preservation of tradition; its disadvantage is the inability which it brings to an individual or to a nation to adapt life to the change of circumstance." Thus we readily fall into the habit of thinking our ways the right ways, the only possible ways for "well-bred" people, or for deeply religious people, or for truly patriotic people. In these ways, prejudice insinuates itself into human relationships.

Primitive Man v. Superman.

Prejudices, blurred vision, rob people of the fruits of thought. Unless we are careful, they make us reflect in our relationships the spirit of primitive man rather than of man as we like to see him—an individual who is perforce a goodly way on the road that leads from the Primitive State to the Country of the Superman. Thought in itself may be a prejudice—in favour of human progress, but that by the way. There are people who glory in their prejudices. They do not see them for what they are, but they think of them as evidence of superiority. "I do not care what

you say, I think ——" is a common abbreviation
of a prejudiced statement.

Thought, of course, can bolster up prejudice,
but it is thought that is narrowed, jaundiced, and
shallow rather than wise, healthy, and deep. One
so great as Hazlitt indirectly endowed prejudice
with high virtue. "No wise man," he said, "can
have a contempt for the prejudices of others; and
he should even stand in a certain awe of his own,
as if they were aged parents and monitors. They
may in the end prove wiser than he."

One of the greatest of our contemporary writers,
John Galsworthy, gets nearer the truth in his
preface to *The Island Pharisees* when he writes:
"The institutions of this country, like the institutions of all other countries, are but half-truths;
they are the working, daily clothing of the nation;
no more the body's permanent dress than is a
baby's frock. Slowly but surely they wear out,
or are outgrown, and in their fashion they are
always thirty years at least behind the fashions
of those spirits who are concerned with what shall
take their place. The conditions that dictate our
education, the distribution of our property, our
marriage laws, amusements, worship, prisons, and
all other things, change imperceptibly from hour
to hour; the moulds containing them, being in-
elastic, do not change, but hold on to the point
of bursting, and then are hastily, often clumsily,

enlarged." These "advantages" are the raw material of our prejudice. They are permanently with us. The mental attitude that we adopt towards them is important. It has been picturesquely asserted that "reasoning against a prejudice is like fighting against a shadow; it exhausts the reasoner, without visibly affecting the prejudice." (Mildmay.) But prejudice is a cancer that needs the surgeon's knife, and unless reasoning in the right way on adequate material can successfully operate, it is difficult to see how the operation can be performed.

QUEERNESS

"THERE'S nowt so queer as folk" is an inelegant but forceful saying that expresses an interesting fact. Life is full of interest. To vary it is the recurring aim of all. Monotony is deadly. Change is the tonic that is needed to give zest to play and purpose to work. The force of example is powerful, and subconsciously it moulds all lives, but there are wide disparities. No two persons are identical, and yet all come under common influences and many have similar aims. People are ready imitators. Imitation is allied to the forces of example. Fortunately for the human race, there is a constant reaching out to self beyond self in the interests of progress. Conceptions of progression—and retrogression—are not always sound.

The significant fact in this connection, though, is that when an individual really believes that a certain action is the right action to take, the highest act of which he is capable is to endeavour to put belief into practice. If we never acted without a guarantee of the rightness of our action we should never get far from a state of inactivity that would closely resemble the inanimate. To think and to do are two of the primary facts of life, though it is impossible to maintain the perfect balance that would eliminate any necessity to retrace our steps. Life has often to be lived on the trial and error method. We act in given ways because we believe that action will bring the desired—and requisite—solution. Action is stimulated by intensity of opinion that requires to be expressed in action. Conviction of the rightness of the opinion should be the basis of action. Opinions held and actions undertaken give people their individual qualities, the totality of which makes each person unique. These differences give rise to both pain and pleasure. From these facts there is no escape.

Truth to Self.

The sincerity of one person is a source of admiration to some and a violent irritant to others. Such a result is inevitable and unavoidable. We copy the examples that we think are worth copying and, assuming the desire to live progressively, resist or try to resist the influence of evil examples. Clash of interests, divergencies in points of view, opposition in action, are seldom absent for long. Throughout there must be truth to self.

"Every one must, of course, think his own opinions right ; for if he thought them wrong, they would no longer be his opinions; but there is a wide difference between regarding ourselves as infallible, and being firmly convinced of the truth of our creed. When a man reflects on any particular doctrine, he may be impressed with a thorough conviction of the improbability or even impossibility of its being false; and so he may feel with regard to all his other opinions, when he makes them objects of separate contemplation. And yet when he views them in the aggregate, when he reflects that not a single being on the earth holds collectively the same, when he looks at the past history and present state of mankind, and observes the various creeds of different ages and nations, the peculiar modes of thinking of sects and bodies and individuals, the notions once firmly held, which have been exploded, the prejudices once universally prevalent, which have been removed, and the endless controversies which have distracted those who have made it the business of their lives to arrive at the truth; and when he further dwells on the consideration that many of these, his fellow-creatures, have had a conviction of the justness of their respective sentiments equal to his own, he cannot help the obvious inference, that in his own opinion it is next to impossible that there is not an admixture of error; that there is an infinitely greater probability of his being wrong in some than right in all."

An Everyday Text.

This Gospel of Toleration, as set forth by the late Viscount Morley in *On Compromise*, is the sort of text that can usefully be kept before all people every day. It applies to the small things as well as the big things of life—and even here what one thinks is small, another thinks is great. We can never be certain about the final resting place of ultimate truth. Man has not discovered it, and until it is discovered man, sometimes strongly against inclination or desire, is driven to acceptance of the fact that all people are of the one species, but that no two members of the species are quite the same. Acceptance, however, is not enough. It should lead to toleration over the differences that are revealed in life. They are all explicable, it is reasonable to assume, though in some cases an explanation has not been discovered.

Queerness in people is a divergence from the normal that creates many and varied reactions in other people. Queer people are "odd, singular, droll." The causes of their queerness may be within their complete control, but the probability is that their queerness will be observable expression of an individual make-up for which they are not wholly responsible. Heredity plays fanciful tricks and leaves legacies that are greatly varied. Environment can and does work in mysterious ways of which we are not wholly conscious until we are the victims, fortunate or unfortunate, of its influences.

Geniuses and Their Lives.

There are people who are non-observers of social functions who regard as queer folk any who are unconventional; routinists look upon the people who act on the spur of the moment as queer; Bohemians are queer in the eyes of those who order their lives in accordance with rule-of-thumb methods. These differing valuations of the desirable in life provide matter for interesting speculation. Was Wagner's queerness in so far as his relations with people were concerned part of the make-up that was essential to the expression of his musical genius? Were the queer antics of Berlioz in love an ineradicable part of his nature? Was Beethoven's bad temper the inevitable concomitant of a master mind in music, the result of poverty, disease, and deafness, or merely the queerness that often accompanies genius?

Although everything we do can be paralleled by what is done by others, the effect upon ourselves is the thing that counts. Queerness can be a distinguishing mark as well as a mark that disfigures. The eccentric but humble individual is queer not less than the man of genius. Both are away from the normal, which in this respect is the standardized, and once that break-away is effected a danger arises of being thought queer by people who have not been or are not guilty of a similar break-away. " I do not know how he can do such a thing," "She ought to be ashamed of herself," and like expressions, in which criticism is implied, are the reactions of people who see queerness in the conduct of others. Probably, in the majority of cases, the people so criticized, even though they are made aware of the criticisms, proceed in accordance with their whims, tastes, fancies, moods, and desires. For these are some of the seeds of queerness.

Unattainable Uniformity.

The oddness of the criminal needs to be avoided, the singularity of the insane is, alas, a great misfortune that all would avoid if they could, but apart from these two violent departures from the normal, constituting as they do unavoidable diseases rather than diseases that are deliberately courted, there are manifold expressions of queerness that give life its touches of romance, its picturesqueness, its infinite variety, which intermittently increases the number of opportunities for healthy development.

But there is no effective point in being queer for the mere sake of being different. Queerness should have its interpretation on a much higher level of values. Queerness that is open to legitimate suspicion, that is obviously debased, should be eschewed, and can be eschewed without blindly ignoring the basic fact that complete uniformity in many walks of life is unattainable. Queerness in the final analysis is one facet of individuality, and it is the quality of the individuality that is of high importance. Reflect upon the points made by J. E. Turner, M.A., Ph.D., in *Personality and Reality*. He states: "The mark of every great personality is individuality in its real sense—the firm combination of knowledge and feelings, of will and purposes, each of which taken by itself covers a wide range, but which none the less forms a persistent unity, capable of facing every emergency of life and of defying all its hostile forces. Such a capacity, it is true, is usually exhibited in only one main direction—in intellectual or artistic power, in practical ability or moral and religious insight; and yet these frequently go together, being seldom found quite lacking in any of the great historic figures of the world; most particularly in the last-mentioned instances can we discern keen sensitivity united with a comprehensive intellectual grasp of an intricate situation; for we must not here restrict 'intellect' to mere book knowledge or systematic education." Queerness is one of the ways in which "individuality in its real sense" manifests itself. We

125

need not then apologize for queerness as such, but the queerness that is indicative of wasted and misused opportunities, of false values and of blinded susceptibilities to uplifting influences and forces, should perturb us.

No. 18

RESISTANCE

THE readiness with which resistance is offered gives a clue to the quality of a person's character. The spirit of resistance is common to all, but it is used differently because people whose guiding principles are fundamentally different hold conflicting opinions on the value of resistance in life. External circumstances inevitably give scope for the exercise of the power of resistance. Some people readily offer the resistance that they think is wanted to deal with circumstances of the moment; other people by similar circumstances are merely strengthened in a mental state that is crystallized in determination to resist the invitation to offer resistance.

The psycho-analyst thinks of resistance as "the instinctive opposition which one displays towards unconscious processes that are in danger of being laid bare." The social reformer, keen in his altruistic well-doing, sees in the delinquencies of people who are the subjects and objects of his reformist activities, moral instabilities, mental torpor, lack of a sound sense of values, which are intensified by taking the "line of least resistance," when it seems that resistance would tend to strengthen the moral fibre, give life to thought, and clarify vision so that human manifestations of life in their great variety would be seen in a truer and consequently a better perspective. But social reformers, whose motives may or may not lack a sound scientific basis, are in a category far different from that of people who apply principles of psychology in certain ways that are explained by their adherence to principles of Christianity, for "In subjective Christian psychology, non-resistance is claimed as the keynote of happiness. 'Resist not evil' is taken to mean that evil becomes such (or becomes greater) when endowed by the consciousness of the percipient with a belief in its reality. It is known in everyday life that the best way to nullify say, teasing, is to take sides with the teaser." (*Our Minds and Our Motives*.)

Perplexities and Variations.

The perplexities and variations in life give life much of its interest. A set of facts can be clearly stated and clearly understood by large numbers of people of average intelligence—absolute equality in all respects would not be a characteristic of a group of any dozen people who can be brought together. Endeavour to realize the principles of absolute equality by bringing together a dozen professors of the same age with similar training and experience, state in unequivocal language the set of facts, and the interpretation will reveal marked differences—and probably strong individual characteristics. (It is understood, of course, that the facts are not ludicrously elementary.) This inability to interpret observed and accepted facts in universally acceptable manner gives life not only its colour and pleasure, but also its drabness and pain. A person with a philosophic turn of mind will proceed on his way unperturbed by circumstances that will give rise to the blackest pessimism in the non-philosophic and even overwhelm them.

Facing Life.

One business man (this is a statement of fact) was engaged on a motor track that had almost been completed when severe weather completely destroyed all the work that had been done and involved him in certain loss of hundreds of pounds and bankruptcy. The work was urgent—completion was essential by the following day because of ceremonial celebrations—and the firm inquired what was to be done. "I am going to have a whiskey and soda" was the reply of the employer, who was "a straight and strict" business man. He faced the inevitable bankruptcy sequel, started again, and became even more successful than he had ever been. Another business man (this is also a statement of fact), successful and wealthy, was asked what he would do if fortune turned and he became unsuccessful and poor. "Commit suicide," he replied, thus revealing an attitude of mind that was unhealthy, whatever his action would have been had unfortunate circumstances arisen. These descriptions have a bearing on resistance.

"Resist Not Evil."

In finality resistance or non-resistance is created by the manner in which we interpret facts, by the philosophy of action (or inaction) that we formulate or that is formulated by others out of the material of life. Interesting and profitable speculation can follow recognition of the fact that there are people, mentally alert, clear thinking, and undoubtedly sincere, who thoroughly believe in the maintenance of a policy the spirit of which is "resist not evil." We are aware that "there is evil in every human heart, which may remain latent; perhaps through the whole of life; but circumstances may rouse it to activity." Moreover, every individual is capable of evil. So far general agreement may not be difficult to obtain, though agreement about the evil itself, unless it be of the glaring kind that must be recognized as such by all normal people, may create difficulties. Relate ideas of the desirability or the undesirability of resistance to evil, and conflict is certain if large numbers of people are primarily concerned.

Fox dogmatically asserted: "There is a spirit of resistance implanted by the Deity in the breast of man, proportionate to the size of the wrongs he is destined to endure." This assertion will not be accepted by some, by those who will look upon it as too fatalistic. Struggle and development are common expressions of life. They are often regarded as highly desirable companions, the one affecting the other with the rhythmic swing of a pendulum. A belief in resistance or in non-resistance can be effective—but a great deal depends upon conditions. A paradox creeps in. Is pacificism, the resistance of war, anything more than militarism, the resistance to others who are bent upon war-making? Can human beings altogether escape resistance to influential forces? The universal truth is as elusive here as it is elsewhere.

There are forces that are too powerful for human beings successfully to resist, even though the will to resist attains in each individual its maximum power. Crowd psychology can teach useful lessons when resistance is thought of in this way. Each person is a compound. Here the emotions become the mainspring of activity; there the intellect is supreme. The respective strengths of spirit, mind, and body reveal themselves time and again, and it would be idle to attempt to resist the revelations.

The Perfect Man.

The individual who can not only control himself absolutely under all conditions, but who can also absolutely control all the conditions that will enter into his life has not yet been born. When he is, he will be the first perfect man. There must be a sifting and a sorting of ideas, a weighing of the pros and cons of diverse actions, and sincerity in the stands that are taken "for" and "against" resistance, for resistance there must be in some form or other. "The line of least resistance" may be a marked line of expediency; to take advantage of the expedient will have an effect or effects, but what it or they will be none can say with a finality that is certain. The day of the prophet is not yet, and it is about as far as human beings can go to say that certain results will accrue if certain factors operate or cease to operate—but the factors themselves, being the stuff of life, are charged with the uncertainties of life.

In many of the practical affairs of life it is obvious, taking the perspective of the moment, that to resist will sometimes be advantageous and sometimes disadvantageous. Reasoning people, intent upon rationalizing their activities as far as is practicable when confronted with these affairs, restrict their reasoning and make up their minds upon the best course to take in the given circumstances. But, in addition to these mundane interests, there are things of the spirit that are the sources of difficulties, often great, sometimes insuperable. Thinking people who are anxious to do right in accordance with their ideas of rightness, and who conscientiously try, are, upon occasions, also conscious of committing acts that their inner conscience says at the time the acts are being done should not be done. The underlying truth of this common human experience is well stated by W. Tudor Jones, D.Phil., in *The Spiritual Ascent of Man*. Having pointed out that the theoretical *Ought* of our judgments about facts, like the practical *Ought* of Ethics is, after all, definable only in terms of what Kant called the Autonomy of the Will, he states: "I *Ought* to do that which I even now, by implication, *mean to do*. My Ought is my own will more rationally expressed than at the instant of a capricious activity I as yet consciously recognize. The consciousness of a more rational purpose—of a purpose looming up, as it were, in the distance, beyond my present impulses, and yet even now seen as their culmination, like a mountain crowning the ascent from the foothills—the consciousness, I say, of such a purpose, is what we mean in Ethics by the Ought. The Ought may appear foreign, but yet it is never at once the Ought and still something wholly foreign to my own will. Constraint, as such, is never moral obligation. The Ought is another will than my impulse, yet it is one with my own meaning, and it expresses more fully and rationally what my impulse even now implies. But if the practical Ought of Ethics is thus the fuller determination of my own will, viewed at once as mine and yet as superior to my present capricious and imperfect expression of my purpose, the theoretical Ought of our present discussion of the categories of Experience is similarly related to the theoretical aspect of my present conscious activity." Resistance or nonresistance can strengthen character and be spiritually energizing. The time to answer, without any qualification, which is better in *all* circumstances, has not yet arrived.

No. 19

SINCERITY

SINCERITY is the touchstone of reality in life.
When we are convinced that a person is sincere
in thought and in action, we feel that we really
know the person. Knowledge is not necessarily
complete, for no person completely knows another
person, and sincerity does not demand complete
revelation. It does, however, guarantee that in
whatever is said there is no substratum of falsity
and that in whatever is done there is no deception.
We can place little or no reliance on what an
insincere person says, or promises, or undertakes,
because remarks drop lightly off the tongue,
promises are scattered as leaves before the wind,
and undertakings are cursory and haphazard.

Sincerity is the distinguishing mark of a person
who has, at any rate, got one solid, substantial
plank in the platform of life. It makes for purity.
Even when we are compelled to disagree with
things that are held and expressed in all sincerity
by people with whom we disagree, sincerity sim-
plifies the position by deepening our understanding. The insincere are triflers. They tamper with
truth. They are too narrow in vision, too shallow
in thought. The importance of sincerity gives it

high place in any carefully compiled list of human attributes.

Sincerity and Happiness.

Confucius firmly linked sincerity and faith, and endowed them with the superlative: they are "the highest thing." Buddha saw in sincerity the guide to personal happiness: "If a man speaks or acts with a pure thought, happiness follows him like a shadow that never leaves him." This is one reason in favour of sincerity, for life without happiness is as an untenanted house. But the mere attainment of happiness is not the sole object of any well ordered life. The pursuit of happiness can be egoism rampant: much depends upon the underlying reason for the pursuit and upon the quality and influences of the happiness that is attained. At the same time, the happy person whose happiness is derived from expression through purity of thought and action has gone far in sound development. Sincerity has other grounds of justification. The sincere by their sincerity furnish proof of a helpful sensitiveness. They lift human relationships on to a higher plane than can be reached by triflers with truths, by people who neither think ahead nor act on well considered lines to advance themselves.

The advance of man is dependent upon man having fixed and worthy ideals of life and conduct, and by man ever striving to build them into life.

Self-Realization and Spiritual Attainment.

Life is many sided, but none of its facets demands insincerity of man. "Self-realization," states Edmond Holmes in *Self-Realization*, "as an ideal, compels one to look beyond the grave, compels one to believe in a plurality of lives, compels one to look forward to an ascent through a succession of lives to higher and still higher levels of self-development, to an advance from grade to grade, from plane to plane, to heights of spiritual attainment which always have higher heights above them. So vast are the potentialities of selfhood that no life, no succession of lives, can suffice for the realization of them." Sincerity is one of life's elevating forces. It helps its adherents and demonstrators to give of their best, whatever that best may be, at any given moment of time. Camouflage, which is considered an essential of war-time and other activities that involve the deception of people by people, is not included in the equipment for life that the sincere find adequate. Their contacts with insincerity are those that are imposed upon them by superior forces and through circumstances that they cannot control. Sincerity is not an attribute that has to be acquired for a specific purpose at any particular moment, used, and then discarded.

Love of Truth.

Scott went awry when he wrote—

> Just at the age 'twixt boy and youth
> When thought is speech, and speech is truth.

These may be the years of sincerity in the sense that during the period that is between childhood and maturity, we are neither infantile nor sophisticated, though in these modern days when the newly acquired liberties of adolescents tend to turn to licence, the period is less easy of precise and concise definition than it was in "the good old days"—a highly disputatious phrase that nevertheless met certain definite requirements. Sincerity is common amongst the young before they become tainted with the sophistications of adult life. They have a spontaneous "love of truth in all its forms" because their immature experience has not convinced them of even temporary advantages of a deviation from the truth. Mature experience should not, of course, carry conviction, but as years pass trials and temptations multiply, and no person is perfect. Just as sincerity is not for use during a rigorously limited period of life but through the whole of life, so it is not inseparable from childhood. There are delinquents of all ages. However, when we pass from childhood we all, in varying measures, run our lives on the rails of reason. Circumstances impel us to leave these rails from time to time;

the fewer the times, the more successfully we exercise the art of true living—if our basic reasoning be sound.

When mental conflicts arise we cannot always decide which is the best of a number of courses to adopt; unforeseen happenings bring us face to face with the necessity to make important changes, but (the citation could be elaborated) there is never a time when, basically, departure from sincerity is justified. Sincerity hall-marks a person's character. It gives it "tone" and distinction, and makes visible the invisible because it reveals attributes of the spirit which can be neither seen nor handled, but which are of greater significance and importance in life than any of the material possessions to obtain which deviations from rectitude are made.

Artificiality and Distortion.

Insincerity in creative art brings artificiality and distortion. Under its influence the creator does not put the best of himself into his art, but less than the best for reasons that at the moment make an irresistible appeal to him. Take the world of the theatre, where in order to create an impression of the actual, the artificial must be introduced. John Galsworthy, one of the most sincere of contemporary playwrights and novelists, in an essay written years ago, asked: "What

then is lying at the back of any growth or development there may have been of late in Drama?"
and replied: "Simply the outcome of sincerity—
of fidelity to mood, of impression to self. A man
here and there has turned up who has imagined
something true to what he had really seen and
felt, and has projected it across the footlights in
such a way as to make other people feel it."
Sincerity, he adds, includes "nothing because it
pays, nothing because it will make a sensation;
no situations faked, no characters falsified; no
fireworks; only something imagined and put down
in a passion of sincerity." John Drinkwater
broadens out thought on these lines in his introduction to St. John Hankin's plays when he
writes: "Ultimately it is sincerity that creates
soul, and sincerity has been lost to our theatre,
save for brief interludes, until these new dramatists once again began to write not from rumour
but from conscience. Those momentarily successful plays that presented life not altogether dis-
torted, and at the same time fulfilled the technical
requirements of the stage, perished because their
virtues were not really sincere. Their makers said
the right thing because it was commonly reported
to be the right thing and not from conviction,
and consequently said it ill, which, artistically,
amounted to not saying it at all. Lacking the
sincerity which should result in style, they lacked

the power of complete utterance, and in art a thing either is completely said or it does not exist."

Aspects of Life.

These are authoritative pronouncements on sincerity in relation to art. With the necessary adjustments, they are equally as applicable to life as people live it day by day as they are to the creative characters that are manipulated by the playwright and that move on the stage to reflect aspects of life. Consciousness, truth, perception, conviction—these are at the root of sincerity. To weave a philosophy of life out of them and other suitable material and to live it to the best of our ability gives sincerity as safe a place as we can ever hope to ensure for it—"Be what you are; let whoso will be what others are. Do not be what you are not, but resolutely be what you can."

No. 20

TACT

ANY person who can say the right thing at the
right time and do the right thing at the right
time is a tactful person. Not all, however, can
easily decide when immediate decision is essential
about the rightness of thing, time, or action.
Afterthoughts are useless. The need of the moment is conditioned by the circumstances of the
moment, and must be met at the time. The outcome of delicate negotiations can be basically
affected by one of the negotiators saying a word
too much or a word too little, by not saying as
much as it is necessary to say, or even by the
manner in which he speaks or maintains silence.
Tact has kinship with manners. It depends upon
the accurate calculation of factors, upon soundness
of judgment. Tact is a demonstration of knowledge. It is not, however, easy of acquirement by
those who have or who appear to have a natural
aptitude for tactlessness.

A knowledge of book-keeping is acquired by the
mastery of basic principles. Once mastery is a
fait accompli, any ordinary book-keeping problem
can be solved by the sound application of those
principles. This applies with equal truth to the

acquirement of various branches of knowledge—
but it is inapplicable to tact. What is right and
what is wrong, the appropriate and the inappro-
priate, the helpful and the harmful, cannot be
definitely taught in the classroom or be mastered
in the privacy of the study so that in all circumstances they can be readily distinguished to enable
sound decision to be reflected in action.

Capacity and Achievement.

The successful journalist has a flair for journalism, an artistic temperament is an indispensable
requisite of the artist, soundness of health and
appropriate specialization give the would-be
athlete the best chance of success, but there must
be latent and suitable capacity before athletic
prominence can be attained. So it is with the
tactful person. Tact can be cultivated, but in
varying degrees, for individual essentials differ.

The tactful person must demonstrate "skill
in handling a difficult position without giving
offence." This is much more easily stated than
demonstration is accomplished. The facts of
everyday life for all persons are rich in possibilities
for good or evil. The root fact, distasteful though
it be to large numbers of sensitive people, is that
involuntary reactions to people and to circumstances vary from individual to individual. Each
of us knows that some types of people "jar,"

though no word be spoken or thing done. They are, in short, unconscious sources of irritation. They disturb the emotional self and make it much more difficult for the disturbed to act normally. Again, when the necessity arises to exchange thoughts, to discuss business or other matters, to counter opinion with opinion, actively to associate in any way with others, there are types that are attractive and types that are repellent, with numerous gradations of states between attractiveness and repellence. With some there is no difficulty in "getting along" smoothly; obstacles are easily overcome, or if they are insuperable there is common understanding of the insuperability and readiness "to agree to differ," while with others even the most simple and innocent relationships quickly become strained for trivial reasons, or harmony is intermittently imperilled by jagged nerves, frayed tempers, unskilful handling of situations, and the like. In the phraseology of theosophists, "auras do not blend." In these and like cases, tact is a valuable asset, but often when it is most wanted by people, although it is not beyond reach, it is not grasped.

An Ingredient of Personality.

Tact is an ingredient of personality. Some people are tactful by nature; tact with them is a positive quality. They are fortunate, for this quality upon which they draw to their own repeated advantage and without effort has to be laboriously acquired by the "bluff, blunt, and brusque," who are frequently confronted with the desirability of subjecting these qualities to vigorous repression in order that tact and charm and delicacy of thought and action in relation to others shall be made influential. But, in all cases, the exercise of thought is from time to time indispensable.

Qualities that go to the making of tact are helpfully summarized by William McDougall (*Character and the Conduct of Life*). "We are apt to think of tact," he writes, "as an inborn or God-given capacity about which nothing more can be said. Yet, clearly, it is not an inborn unitary function; it is a complex resultant of the co-operation of moral and intellectual capacities. First, the man who is to be tactful must have delicate sympathy (in the strict sense) or he will not quickly and surely note the emotional states and reactions of others. Secondly, he must be of quick judgment and decision. The deliberative cautious man will often realize too late how he should have acted. Hence intuition, rather than reasoned judgment, and perfect self-confidence are necessary for tact of a high order. Nevertheless, though these factors of tact are for the most part inborn, tact may, to a certain extent, be cultivated by the average man, if he will constantly keep in view the fact that, by managing men, he can gain his ends more surely than by driving them, that the iron hand is all the more effective when gloved in velvet."

Mingled Intellect and Emotion.

Life's circumstances vary with such persistency that the pros and cons are not always quickly discernible. Analysis has to precede valuation, which must be undertaken before judgment can be delivered. Tact is often wanted during the time these and other processes are operative. It is helpful to keep constantly in mind the conflicting constituents of human nature. "Even the loftiest minds," states Mr. Lothrop Stoddard in *Scientific Humanism*, "are ferments of mingled intellect and emotion, with rational thought distilling itself slowly and sparsely through the cooling medium of conscious endeavour. With the mass of mankind, rational thought is rare, and is easily overwhelmed by floods of primitive passion welling up from the emotional depths." The tactful person, by natural inclination or deliberate design, manages more successfully to control these floods, has a readier and more reliable recognition of the evils that follow the awakening into virility of primitive passion than the tactless person, whose lack of tact is in part explainable by his inability to think right and to think straight at the given moment when readiness and straightness are of importance. He is handicapped not so much by the excess of his emotions as by his failure to keep them in effective control through exercise of thought.

" The amount of disguised emotion to-day masquerading as thought is literally astounding. Nowhere do we see it more plainly than in the current tendency to 'think in phrases'; in other words, to *avoid thinking* by embracing some clever catchword or resounding 'principle' which *seems* to settle the question and bring conviction to perplexed souls. This is a very insidious evil," states Mr. Stoddard, "because it so subtly debauches the intellect and kills creative thought. Constructive thinking is hard work, while nothing is more painful than a disturbing idea. How much simpler to take a mental short-cut which we fondly imagine will do the work and ease the pain!"

Mental Short-Cuts and Shortcomings.

"Mental short-cuts" are cuts to many of our shortcomings. Energetic and ambitious young people, admirable in a number of ways, sometimes and inevitably, for the failure is common, reveal defects of their qualities—energy too vigorously applied, ambition too keenly pressed, strain and warp character. They become inconsiderate, and this is one of the avenues by which tactlessness enters into life. Another is the imposition of authority in harsh, unreasoning fashion. Lack of tact explains not only the presence of inconsideration, but also of other defects that are exhibited by those whose character is not well balanced. Tact is one of the keepers of appropriateness, but it requires to be fitted into a general scheme of life, otherwise it can be made to override other first-rate qualities. Silence that springs from false notions of the importance of tact—for example, when speech is demanded for truth's sake when truth should be told—should not be maintained. Tact must have companionship with skill, and upon occasions intuition will give evidence of the successful exercise of thought related to practice. Tact can be more than talent. The aim should be to make a talent of tact. Attainment involves an alliance of the gifts of intuition and the gifts that are the friends of mental labours.

No. 21

UNDERSTANDING

FERRAND, an alien, is one of the characters introduced by John Galsworthy in *The Pigeon*, a fantasy that brings out the power of understanding, the consequences that flow from lack of understanding, and the difficulties of harmonizing altruistic idealism and the practicalities of everyday life. Ferrand is one of a motley, two others being Timson, once a cabman, and Guinevere Megan, a flower seller. They are befriended by an artist, Christopher Wellwyn, and brought under the observation of a Canon, a Professor, and a Justice of the Peace. Ferrand is of philosophic bent. He philosophizes about life to Wellwyn and, at the same time, reveals his opinions and theories. Here is an illuminating fragment of dialogue—

Wellwyn : We're our own enemies, Ferrand . . .

Ferrand : (earnestly) Monsieur, do you know this? You are the sole being that can do us good—we hopeless ones.

Wellwyn : (shaking his head) Not a bit of it; I'm hopeless too.

Ferrand : (eagerly) Monsieur, it is just that. You *understand*. When we are with you we feel something— here—(he touches his heart). If I had one prayer to make, it would be, Good God, give me to understand! Those sirs, with their theories, they can clean our skins and chain our 'abits—that soothes for them the aesthetic sense; it gives them too their good little importance. But our spirits they cannot touch, for they nevare understand. Without that, Monsieur, all is dry as a parched skin of orange.

This extract, indeed the play as a whole, gives emphasis to human values that are realizable when men and women in their multifarious relationships with one another exercise the power to understand. Understanding is not only of the mind, but also of the spirit. "A healthy understanding," says Carlyle, "is not the logical argumentation, but the intuition: for the end of understanding is not to prove and find reasons, but to know and believe." This, however, does not make understanding an act of faith. Both stimulating and comforting is the fact that what is given by intuition can very often be acquired by deliberate mental effort. More than knowledge, however, is needed. Theorists, as Galsworthy depicts, can know the life-beat of a problem and can apply principles that in cold logic should suffice to provide a solution.

Life and Logic.

Life, however, repeatedly confuses the logicians. In logic, a right start is made with the premises (known truths) and a sound conclusion (other and distinct truths deduced from known truths) is arrived at. Not so with life. Truth expressed in

terms of human life has too many aspects, and
too much may and does happen to make certain
of final conclusions—until they are reached, and
even they may not be what they seem to be!
Life is rich in possibilities and probabilities.

Each individual has different interests. It is
inevitable that all people at all times cannot see
eye to eye with each other. Too often differences
in outlook, in aim, in activities, are condemned.
They require to be understood, for understanding,
which in many cases bestows the capacity to forget, to forgive, to overlook, to tolerate, to sym-
pathize—gives rise to an attitude of mind that
is sincere and sympathetic, that leads to recognition of ineradicable differences in human nature
and of the fundamental right of each individual
(with qualification made requisite by insanity,
heredity, or innate criminal tendencies, and so on)
to live his or her own life.

Life is a mosaic. Each individual contributes
to the pattern, but each individual's contribution
cannot be identical. It must be individualistic.
If this individualism is to be rightly interpreted,
there must be understanding. Individuals, of
course, identify themselves with other individuals
whose tastes are similar, whose aims are identical
—hence local organizations develop into county
movements, spread to national, and, finally,
in these days, to international associations.

Ultimately, however, the influences that are generated by these human links get individualistic interpretations and expressions.

Self-Realization and Human Progress.

Understanding is necessary to give any human being the fullest scope for self-realization and also for human progress in general. Two proverbs crystallize the underlying truth of this necessity. One has it that "Men's best candle is understanding," and the other that it is better to understand the world than to condemn it. The first is a reminder that understanding is a powerful illuminant, and the second contains the suggestion that, though there be grounds for condemnation, understanding will lead to or help forward recognition of the causes that give rise to grounds for condemnation, and that the better course is to pursue the path of understanding rather than to halt to deliver judgment. If we believe, with Schlegel, that understanding is a mechanically, wit a chemically, and genius an organically, acting spirit, we shall, realizing the power of understanding, seek in the first place to master the mechanism which, once in working order, produces understanding. It is a mechanism of the mind that works smoothly when the oils of the emotions and of the spirit are used as lubricants.

We want love as well as knowledge, altruism

as well as justice, to give us true understanding. To attain it, it is often essential to adapt and maintain the trial and error method. It is wrong to assume that knowledge must yield success. Knowledge often comes through failure. If trial be not made, results that come only through successful endeavour remain out of reach. Sometimes to try is to place ourselves in intimate association with the experience of failure. Failure, however, has much to teach. Healthy ambition makes the ambitious, upon occasions, attempt to achieve before they have carried theory and practice sufficiently far in advance of necessity to give reasonable promise of achievement. The formation of bad or wrong habits has also stultifying effects.

The Lesson of Unlearning.

Increased understanding comes in divers ways. One involves the breaking of bad habits. As the years pass we change; a static outlook is evidence of stagnation. There must be both widening and deepening. Before years of discretion, from the point of view of spiritual development, are reached, prejudices may have become strongly rooted. To uproot them may be difficult. It becomes necessary to learn the lesson of unlearning. No normal person can altogether avoid the formation of erroneous or conflicting habits. Any normal person earnestly desirous of seeking to enlarge his or her sphere of understanding will have to break habits—an impracticable task in some cases, but in most cases not too far advanced to resist skilful treatment.

Although theoretically the breaking of habits, states Dr. William H. Burnham in *The Normal Mind*, "may not be possible . . . nevertheless, for practical purposes, it is true that we can break up habitual forms of reaction, and the ability to do this is the mark of health and sanity. Hence, it becomes of importance if not quite as important to study methods of unlearning as to study methods of learning." Habits of mind that tend to make us think of self in superior terms, that give us an urge to make others imitators of ourselves because we wish them to be as we are, that create antagonisms and conflicts, should be broken. Understanding of another's point of view is a powerful aid. Once understand the motives that bring human actions into being, and the spirit of toleration has an excellent chance to thrive.

Root Differences.

Our neighbour lives a different life from that which commends itself to us. He is a "different" social animal. Why? We have a bias in favour of thrift, and on all hands see the practical values that arise from thrifty habits, but others are spendthrifts and will not yield to sincere appeals that are made to them in efforts to make them change their ways. Why? This type of question can easily be multiplied. Answers reveal acceptance of the fact that different people observing different customs, living under the influences of different traditions, having different aims, necessarily evaluate life in different terms, order their lives in accordance with their own ideas of values, and, consequently, both in thought and in action, reach conclusions different from others who are equally gifted in all ways. To understand these root differences is enormously helpful in life.

There must be regulations, disciplinary measures must be drawn up, and for governmental and other purposes must be imposed. The most effective discipline, however, is that imposed from within; the best regulations are those we make for ourselves—when it is understood that we are really never free from the moral necessity to make the most of ourselves. Others can either help or hinder and we can both hinder and help ourselves. External and internal endeavours at improvements must be shot with understanding for them to be effective.

"Leave us to live, or leave us to die when we like in the free air," says Ferrand. Do not let the theorists "make us prisoners, with their theories, because we are not like them—it is life itself they would enclose!" he urges and suggests. Again, "The Good God made me so that I would rather walk a whole month of nights, hungry, with the stars, than sit one single day making round business on an office stool! It is not to my advantage. I cannot help it that I am a vagabond. What would you have? It is stronger than me." There is, of course, insidious danger in merely understanding that "things and people are as they are," and in being satisfied to leave them so. There is, too, danger in systematically attempting to standardize and to mechanize people—things are as the collective efforts of people make them. Understanding built upon true wisdom and buttressed by sound knowledge is the type of edifice that is worthy of erection.

VERSATILITY

VERSATILITY in these days of intensified specialization is an attribute that is admired by many
and practised by a few who, exceptional no doubt,
are impelled to realize themselves upon a particular plane of thought and activity. The industrialization of the age tends to make robots of
people. A robot is one who functions mechanically. Devoid of thought, he (and she) acts according to plan—the plan of another or of others.
The word itself is derived from the Brothers Capek,
whose imaginative treatment, in the play *R.U.R.*,
of the mechanization of life not only gave the
English language a new word, but also the English
and other people stimulating thought on aspects
of the adverse effects of too narrowly restricting
thought and feeling. Rossum's Universal Robots
are admirable utilitarian slaves—until they begin
to think and to feel.

The emphasis to-day is upon specialization in
all branches of human activity. Specialization
makes for high efficiency—but often at a cost that
prompts questionings. Can human beings, who, in
order to gain a livelihood, have to pursue one
highly specialized, monotonous task day by day,

week by week, and month by month, satisfactorily express themselves? Are men and women so resolute that during their leisure they can counteract by self-chosen activities the influences of work that cribs, cabins, and confines the mind and stifles the spirit? Has natural versatility a chance to express itself in these artificial days when life is lived in grooves by many because practical living offers no reasonable escape?

Specialization.

Practicality imposes recognition of the soundness of efficiency. Specialization is very largely habit formulated and consolidated. It makes for economy of effort, for speed in execution. Moreover, it does not necessarily involve monotony or drabness. The worker who must repeat mechanical operations throughout years is not necessarily reduced to the status of an unthinking, non-reflective, human animal. Mechanization of his working life, especially by the introduction of mechanical labour-saving machines and devices, not only enables him considerably to conserve his physical energy, but also in many cases to eliminate mental strain. These, of course, are relevant facts that give adverse critics plausible grounds for roundly condemning contemporary specialization. On the other hand, they are facts that may ultimately be the foundation upon which is built an improved system of vocational selection and leisure-time recreation. The two are more closely related than is suggested by educational systems. Specialization has simplified work and made a problem of the spending of leisure.

The Goodwill of Education.

Educationists are not agreed upon the best form of education, psychologists are endeavouring to work out in practice methods of testing prospective workers so that when work is begun it is the most suitable for the individual worker taking his or her natural endowments, aptitudes, training, and potentialities into consideration, and social welfare workers, politicians, and others are concerned with the ways in which leisure time is used —and misused. Sir John Adams, M.A., B.Sc., LL.D., in *Educational Theories*, touches upon "what is probably the highest form in which the goodwill of education can be presented." He states: "Self-realization implies the making the best of oneself; bringing out of oneself the best of which one is capable. Sometimes the same ideal is represented by the term *self-expression*, but this term is not quite satisfactory. For it implies the existence of a self already made, and ordinary experience shows us that ready-made things are not quite so good as things made to order. A ready-made self is not so attractive as

159

one in the process of making. Further, mere self-expression does not even hint at further development. Self-realization suggests a goal; expression does not. The notion of the ideal underlies the concept of self-realization. Further, it includes the notion of subordination of self to secure higher development for that self."

The industrialization of the twentieth century worker, making of him during a large part of every working day a mechanical specialist, has given significance to this "concept of self-realization." In days gone by the worker was a versatile and efficient craftsman; to-day he is too often a one-groove mechanician. A point of view that has a bearing on this subject is provocatively expressed by Mr. James Harvey Robinson in *The Humanizing of Knowledge.* Undoubtedly, the educationist is one of the most important of all people who are concerned with providing human beings as they grow to adulthood with facilities for living what in common phraseology is termed "a full life."

Rehumanizing Knowledge.

Specialization narrows, though it may deepen. Versatility widens, though it may make for shallowness. "In the enterprise of rehumanizing knowledge it is necessary first to recognize," states Mr. Robinson, "that specialization, so essential in research, is putting us on the wrong track in education. This has been suspected for some time; nevertheless, even the latest scheme of educational reform which reaches me proposes that we continue to classify our instruction under social sciences, natural sciences and language— to which some might be tempted to add, the fine arts. Representatives of these branches are summoned to testify as to the significance and setting that should be assigned to their particular sciences in a new attempt 'to enable our youth to realize what it means to live in society, to appreciate how people have lived and do live together, and to understand the conditions essential to living together well; to the end that our youth may develop such abilities, inclinations, and ideals as may qualify them to take an intelligent and effective part in an evolving society.'"

The effect of education on versatility is considerable. The educational influences of early life persist throughout life. There are people who, thinking in terms of the immediately practical, desire to give undue emphasis to utilitarian aspects of education. Others, recognizing the dangers that are inherent in vocational training too narrowly restricted, stress the importance of cultural aspects of education. The best education that young people can receive during school days is probably the education that makes surest of ultimate individual self-realization. Versatility introduces variety into life, provides opportunities for healthy reactions to circumstances. The versatile person is not necessarily the superficial person ; the dilettante are not the most thorough exponents of versatility or revealers of its values. The worker who has to perform a task that does not call for the exercise of deep thought is not called upon to eschew deep thought. Mental and manual labours can and do run concurrently.

During apparent idleness, various classes of men have ruminated philosophically and imagined to their own advantage in particular and to the general good. A wise answer to the question, "How can leisure be profitably spent?" enables beneficial reactions to influences to be set up to illuminate the lop-sided, and to make possible the maintenance of a healthy balance.

An Outlet and a Safety Valve.

Versatility is both an outlet and a safety valve. When a person does certain things because of practical necessity, they are not always the best things. Leisure time pursuits in many such cases are the means of partial self-realization. They are an outlet. Basically, the character of the outlet is expressive of the character of the individual —thus is his early education strongly linked with post-schooldays. Further, life would be greatly impoverished if it were not for self-made opportunities for leisure-time self-realization, opportunities that constitute safety valves for people who can neither express nor realize individual gifts during working hours. In the general scheme of life there are bound to be round pegs in square holes. The compensation is that if early training and later development are sound natural talents and latent aptitudes get their chances.

Dr. Charles J. Whitby, in *Makers of Man*, which is a study of human initiative, dealing with versatility and adaptability, is illuminating. "Somewhere in the world of established activities," he writes, "the most unique soul will find that specific task begun to which it feels itself drawn by invincible affinities. I do not mean to imply that the matter is quite so simple as a too facile interpretation of the peg-and-hole metaphor might suggest. The one-man-one-capacity hypothesis will not by any means cover the complex actualities of human greatness. The element of versatility has a decided claim to recognition; of many potentialities, not all, in the nature of things, can expect realization. For the development of some, the environmental conditions may be adverse, even prohibitive; others, more opportune, may prosper at their expense. Nor is it even a foregone conclusion that the capacity which finds fruition was originally the dominant central potentiality of the nature. Adaptability is one element of greatness; if need be, it must stoop to conquer. By the law of hedonic selection, persistence in a given course of activity is conditioned by the pleasurable accompaniment of a sense of difficulties overcome—of some kind or degree of success."

A Channel for Self-Expression.

"Thwarted efforts tend to be relinquished in favour of others whose issue is, or seems likely to be, more favourable. This consideration obviously complicates the problem of natural vocation, raising, among others, the question whether a man, who in a bygone age achieved fame as a poet or painter, might not, if born in our time, have invaded the field of science or speculation. Leonardo's, is, in my opinion, a case in point: he was versatile to the degree of universal potentiality, and it is quite an open question whether the line he chose, or I should say accepted, was that most suited for the full development of his powers." Versatility is not capricious emotions or spasmodic activities that are created by whims and fancies, blind and purposeless. It is a channel by means of which individual qualities are expressed.

No. 23

WISDOM

"WISDOM," said Rochefoucauld, "is to the soul what health is to the body." It is the key that we must consult, upon which we must rely, when the textbook of life becomes difficult and obscure. If our mental gifts are superior to the average, and if they are used with an abundance of energy that springs from intensity of desire, wisdom is not ours unless we are facile in the right use of knowledge, irrespective of the manner of its acquirement. Just as toleration is the foundation of sympathy, so wisdom is the inseparable companion of understanding.

The wise are the spiritually perceptive. Wisdom is not synonymous with knowledge. A man can carry special study to such lengths that he becomes as an encyclopaedia in comparison with the non-studious, who, as it were, continue to struggle with the mastery of the alphabet of life, but, unless he can use his encyclopaedic knowledge in ways that reflect keen and sure perception of spiritual aspects of life he will not demonstrate wisdom, though he will repeatedly impress with the weight of his knowledge.

Ability satisfactorily to perform a given task may be undoubted; to decide in favour of or against the performance may call for the exercise of wisdom. We soon learn that we cannot buy knowledge. It must be acquired. Sound acquirement can be tested. For example, examinations are part of the educational system. Various classes of students are many; professional workers have to study in order to qualify themselves for occupational pursuits. Their study is specialized. Their aim is to acquire theoretical and practical knowledge. At given stages, their knowledge is tested in the examination room where it is possible to ascertain with precision the extent and quality of the knowledge that has been acquired and that is applied in the examination room. This system of testing is not perfect. The conditions in the examination room, the whole circumstances of examination, may prejudicially affect candidates, so that they do themselves less than justice—hence criticism, which is fundamentally sound, of the examination system. Nevertheless, in the given circumstances, knowledge can be tested; the drawback is that these circumstances may never be repeated. So it is with life generally. The world is the examination room. We are the candidates. Each day we make additions to knowledge, and each day little bits of knowledge crumble away. Knowledge is diverse, and it is needed for many purposes. By the application of knowledge we live; by imperfect and unwise use of knowledge we create life's difficulties and problems.

Wisdom a Solvent.

Wisdom is a solvent. It cannot be bought except in the school of experience, in the classroom that gives understanding. It follows that it can be taught—by precept and example, but the effectiveness of the teaching depends upon the aptitude of the pupil. The wise deliberately do things that their wisdom tells them should be taboo. We can all, upon occasions, be wiser in thought than in action. We flout wisdom and indulge self. Because this is natural we cannot safely allow such an attitude unchecked development. Only by rigorous self-discipline can man advance. This is indisputable, but from time to time, owing to man's frailties, the indisputability can be evaded. The onward march cannot proceed uninterruptedly. It is helpful to recognize the fact—and it is perhaps more helpful to keep clearly in mind the destination. All are not suitable for vigorous marching.

The soundness of the training as well as the quality of the physique of soldiers is revealed by endurance tests. It is similar with life apart from the route march and the sham battle manoeuvres.

We are all soldiers in the sense that we have to fight. Some of the sternest battles that we are engaged in are with ourselves, and sometimes we can intelligently anticipate defeat—in those tests when the will to do is more strongly assertive than the determination to give living force to our own highest wisdom in terms of practicality. To think thus of wisdom conveys an idea of the difficulties that must confront any human being who is seriously desirous of being consistently wise. Napoleon would not admit the inevitability of the impossible. He was unwise in his day and time, and the harvest, grown from the seeds of folly, was garnered during his lifetime. The folly is to think that we can always be supremely wise, and our wisdom lies in our sharpness in recognizing that as we go through life we must rub shoulders with folly.

Mastery of Self.

Rigorous self-disciplinary measures persistently maintained serve to act as a brake upon the wheels of life when they revolve in the direction opposite to that taken by wisdom. We must learn to master ourselves in so far as our own voluntary acts are concerned before we can get ourselves on the best vantage point to understand others, and, understanding, learn to associate with them wisely and well. The subjective life

must be understood and controlled to the limits
of true understanding and sound controlment if
the foundation of wisdom is to be well and truly
laid.

All, indeed, can helpfully take to heart and
mind a few of the meditations of Marcus Aurelius:
"Spend not the remnant of thy days in thoughts
and fancies concerning other men, when it is not
in relation to some common good, when by it
thou art hindered from some other better work.
That is, spend not thy time in thinking, what
such a man doth, and to what end: what he saith,
and what he thinks, and what he is about, and
such other things or curiosities, which make a
man to rove and wander from the care and observation of that part of himself, which is rational,
and overruling. See therefore in the whole series
and connexion of thy thought, that thou be careful to prevent whatsoever is idle and impertinent:
but especially, whatsoever is curious and malic-
ious: and thou must use thyself to think only
of such things, of which if a man upon a sudden
should ask thee, what it is that thou art now
thinking, thou mayest answer This, and That,
freely and boldly, that so by thy thoughts it may
presently appear that in all thee is sincere, and
peaceable; as becometh one that is made for
society, and regards not pleasures, nor gives way
to any voluptuous imaginations at all: free from

all contentiousness, envy, and suspicion, and from whatsoever else thou wouldest blush to confess thy thoughts were set upon." This is the quintessence of idealizing the counsel of perfection. It is at once a stimulus to self-discipline and a measure by which inadequacy of spiritual possessions is ascertained. Freedom from "all contentiousness, envy, and suspicion," and elimination of "whatsoever else thou wouldest blush to confess thy thoughts were set upon" are unattainable ideals, and yet every step made in the direction of freedom and elimination is a step towards greater wisdom.

Inescapable Influences.

Self-control must be exercised when a number of questions have to be answered, questions that are concerned with actions. On all hands are influences that impinge upon what we would do or what we think it right to do. The ways in which we respond to or resist those influences are in actuality our answers to those questions. They are, too, representatives of the wisdom that is in us. Self-control helps to perfect the subjective life; it also gives a perspective to objective life. That perspective is ever changing. That ripening knowledge gives a ripening of understanding. A passage in Schopenhauer's notebook emphasizes this point: "A child has no

conception of the inexorableness of natural laws
and the inflexible persistency of everything to
its own entity. The child thinks even lifeless
things will bend a little to his will, because he
feels himself at one with Nature, or because he
believes it friendly towards him through ignorance
of the spirit of the world. . . . It is only after
mature experience that we realize the inflexibility
of human characters, which no entreaties, no
reasoning, no examples, no benefits can change;
how on the contrary, every human being follows
out his own manner of action, his own way of
thought, and his own capabilities with the un-
erringness of a natural law, so that whatever you
try to effect he will remain unchanged."

To impart experience makes for an increase in
wisdom if life is lived purposefully towards the
attainment of idealistic ends. There is an inevitability about natural laws, an unwillingness or dis-
ability to change, and yet all is change. Wisdom
of thought does not necessarily develop concurrently with an extension of knowledge. Wisdom
of action is not the inevitable successor to wisdom
of thought. First, perhaps, there must be knowledge. Natural gifts require qualification. Latent
tendencies have to materialize ere they are fully
vitalized for good or evil. The pursuit of knowledge interests most intelligent people, but their
motives are often poles apart.

The Stream of Life.

It is easier to become interested in life's super-
ficialities than in life's profundities. To know,
through books or by actual contact, something
of many trivialities is to possess knowledge, but
such knowledge is not on the same plane as that
which is gained by endeavour to keep alert and
to maintain a sense of direction, of poise, of ultimate destination, in the main currents of the
stream of life. The obstacles are many; there
must be obstructions. The knowledge that is
derived from adoption and maintenance of an
enlightened attitude towards self and others is
the knowledge which, rightly used, enables man to
reach the highest heights of wisdom. Mistakes are
unavoidable, but by mistakes we learn, and when
we learn we grow, learn to grow so that we never
cast aside "some common good" when we see it
is, in fact, self-growth that helps to revitalize the
spirit. Wisdom is knowledge and understanding
in action. "Growth," it has been said, "is the
wisest man's greatest delight—growth in physical
strength, growth in knowledge, and in mental
power." The application of sound knowledge in
accordance with the spirit of true understanding
makes for growth. Man can never act beyond
the range of his powers, but he can continue to
increase those powers throughout life. To give the
threefold aspects of life (physical, mental, and

spiritual) every chance for useful service on their respective planes and to make daily action conform to the highest conception of duty to self and to our neighbours, are the paths that man must tread for wisdom to keep pace with ever-increasing knowledge.

XENOMANIA

XENOMANIA is defined as "abnormal liking for
things foreign." Both word and definition are no
doubt "foreign" to large numbers of well-educated
people. Most of us do not need the word as an
essential part of our reading, writing, or speaking
vocabulary. It is not in everyday currency—
like many other words that are expressive of root
ideas. It is a common failing to be satisfied with
the minimum number of words that are more or
less adequate for ordinary things rather than to
till the rich fields of the English (and other)
languages. In one of Mr. W. J. Locke's novels
we read that "We have the richest language that
ever a people accreted and we use it as if it were the
poorest. We hoard up our infinite wealth of words
between the boards of dictionaries and in speech
dole out the worn bronze coinage of our vocabulary. We are the misers of philological history."
(*Morals of Marcus Ordeyne*.) The *Oxford English
Dictionary* contains a record of 414,825 words, of
which the average individual makes daily use of
only a small proportion. But this by the way.

Xenomania is a word that is certain to be more
and more pressed into everyday service as the idea
that gives rise to it becomes, as it is becoming,

more extensively popular, or, in the spirit of modern journalism and of modern style in written and spoken expression, a shorter word will supersede it and yet be its synonym.

Normality and Abnormality.

"An abnormal liking for things foreign" is in itself not necessarily bad. There are many reasons why all healthy citizens of any country should be satisfied to keep as near as is practicable to the normal. To be normal is to be "safe." Normality does not raise problems; abnormality gives rise to many, some of which there is a normal disinclination to face. The abnormal when born must live. Must? Well, who shall say in what manner abnormality may express itself.

In music, were Beethoven, Wagner, and Berlioz normal? In statesmanship, Elizabeth, Charles I, and Cromwell? In literature, Shelley, Tolstoi, and Strindberg? Among contemporaries, are Mussolini, Bernard Shaw, and the Sitwells? Legalize the extermination of the abnormal (if ascertainable) at birth and geniuses as well as idiots will meet with early deaths.

These side glances at abnormality can be coupled with the Xenomaniacs whose "abnormal liking for things foreign" is being variously considered. The patriot has what up to now has been accepted as a "normal liking for things native."

175

Patriotism is difficult to explain. As with the artistic temperament and other hereditary endowments, some have it in abundance and some seem to know it not. Those who have it strongly find it impossible wholly to eradicate it, and those who are without it do not find it easy to cultivate. Love of native country not only seems to be natural; it is. It is as natural and sometimes it is easier for the native to love his native country as it is for him to love his father and his mother, his sisters and his brothers. The springs of this natural love are hidden. Their yield is abundant and is capable of being lashed into fury. And there's the rub! There is always the converse for shadow, and because statesmen and politicians, industrialists, and others have recurringly tried to evade the shadow that is thrown by patriotism in violent action, patriotism itself has impelled men to disastrous engagements. Thus, in the words of Nurse Edith Cavell, "Patriotism is not enough."

Ideas—New and Old.

Old ideas must give place to new. To be able to indulge in rapturous appreciation of the good things of the land of our birth should not blind us to the good things that are foreign. "My country right or wrong" is, in the ultimate, as irrational a stand to take as it is possible for human beings to take, and equally as ludicrous as would be the personal proclamation of superiority, "Myself right or wrong." None of us is always right. There are times when correction is possible, and when it should be permissible. Similarly, there is no citizen of any country whose country is always right, and to declare oneself willing to stand by the wrong is to belittle the stature of man as a reasoning animal and to abdicate in favour of intellectual dishonesty. To pursue this line of thought, however, is unnecessary when reflecting upon xenomania and its expressionists.

There are "things foreign," which, like abnormality, make for sound development upon general lines. Goethe in some of his writing pointed the finger at what was, and indicated what might be—if width as well as depth of vision and feeling were cultivated. "We cannot always," he said, "avoid what is foreign; what is good often lies so far off. A true German cannot abide the French, and yet he will drink their wine with the utmost relish." Here is reminder of the absurd over-accentuation of national traits.

Points of view change with the passing of time. If the true British patriot could live as long as the He-Ancient in Shaw's *Back to Methuselah*, he would be confronted with the task, so very difficult of accomplishment according to individual circumstances, of hating or loving, respecting or reviling, the true patriots of sundry other nations—

unless fundamental changes in habits of thought that are beginning to appear are developed and lived. Goethe was in advance of the general thought of his day when, writing on the same theme, he stated: "People that are like-minded can never for any length be disunited; they always come together again; whereas those that are not like-minded try in vain to maintain harmony; the essential discord between them will be sure to break out some day."

World Harmony.

The maintenance of a world harmony remains one of man's unfinished tasks. Disliking things foreign, he has in the past been the unfortunate victim of his rulers who have been able to play, for motives pure and impure, upon his dislikes. It is possible that a system of national education that had for basic object the cultivation among pupils of all classes of an "abnormal liking for things abnormal" would be a potent factor in bringing about world peace. World-war is possible because of a lack of understanding, because the peoples of one country can be misrepresented to the peoples of any other country. Insularity has been paramount for ages. Its supremacy is now dangerously threatened by the march of modern science. It is no longer possible to maintain sensible poise and to think insularly.

Improved and improving methods of transporta-
tion have taken village to town and town to city.
Parochialism in the dim past was what nationalism
is to-day. The one had to go; the other must go
if humanity is to prove itself master of the mighty
forces that it has created. Mr. H. G. Wells is one
of the most persistent and imaginative propagandists of the idea of the inevitability of the
World State. "I would compare what is happen-
ing to the human species," he states in *The World
of William Clissold,* "with what happens to an
insect that undergoes a complete metamorphosis.
Man was a species living in detached and separated
communities; he is now being gathered together
into one community. He is becoming one great
co-operative interplay of life which is replacing
a monotony of individual variations. He is changing in every social relationship and developing a
new world of ideas and mental reactions, habits
of mind and methods of feeling and action, in
response to the appeal of the new conditions.
Nature, I take it, is impartial and inexorable. He
is no specially favoured child. If he adapt he
passes on to a new phase in the story of life; if
he fail to solve the riddles he faces now he may
differentiate, he may degenerate, he may die out
altogether. One thing Nature will not endure of
him: that he stay as he is. I do not regard the
organization of all mankind into one terrestrial

anthill, into Cosmopolis, the greater Athens, the Rome and Paris and London of space and time, as a Utopian dream, as something that fantastically might be. I regard it as the necessary, the only possible, continuation of human history."

A World Republic.

Again, "As the new order struggles to assure itself against a repetition of the disaster of 1914, and is forced towards self-realization in the effort, its peculiar characteristics become plainer. The world republic is going to be as different from any former state as, let us say, an automobile from a peasant's cart. Its horse-power will be in its body. There need be no visible animal, no emperor nor president at all; and no parliament of mankind. It is an anthropomorphic delusion that a state must have a head. A world republic needs a head no more than a brain needs a central master neuron. A brain thinks as a whole."

Theorizing in this vein takes thoughts far beyond the pros and cons of xenomania and yet "abnormal liking for things foreign" in comparison with the normalities of contemporary life is a stage through which human beings will have to pass in their onward march. An "abnormal liking for things native" leads many Englishmen who must travel to rely upon their knowledge, often inadequate, of their native tongue. To indulge an abnormal liking for a foreign language—innocent indulgence indeed—is to begin to pave the way for a deeper and truer understanding of the people whose language is mastered, especially if mastery be the prelude to the study of foreign literature—fictional, historical, biographical, political, sociological—and to a free mixing and mingling that can be fully experienced only when there are no barriers of oral communication to overcome.

Many Ways.

As an expert linguist, Mr. P. G. Wilson, M.Sc., has pertinently written: "If you stay at home, you will let yourself be bound by the local or national conventions and never see the hollowness of them. You will judge harshly anyone who cuts up his meat with his knife, and then lays it down on the table whilst he plies his fork for the rest of the meal. There will be only one proper, decent way of eating—your way! But, if you hob-nob with other nationalities, you will see that there are many ways, and you will not worry about how a man cuts up his meat so long as he is an interesting human being. National customs and national prejudices will interest you, but will not make you wince nor sneer. The well-bred Dutchman would not dream of being so impolite as to rise up from his chair and offer it to a lady, because, he will gravely explain, the chair is warm!

It simply is not done! And he will not understand your laughter at this, to you, quaint custom. When in Germany, you raise your hat to a lady before she greets you; in England you wait until she deigns to recognize you. The German shows his politeness by saluting the lady, the Englishman by allowing her the choice of his acquaintanceship. But both are polite! In France, the lady always walks on your left so that your sword-arm shall be free to defend her; in England you walk on the outside so that you can, if necessary, step off into the gutter! *Toujours la politesse!* In England there are certain human activities that we avoid in conversation; abroad they are taken as a matter of course. Are we ultra-prudish? Are they coarse? It depends on the point of view! Why not enjoy both points of view? When you first leave your native country, you are quite convinced that the English you speak is Standard English, but as you travel round the Continent and ask, say in Tours, where is the best French spoken, and are told 'In Tours,' and in Bordeaux are told 'In Bordeaux,' and, if you further find that in all the provinces they heartily and unanimously condemn Parisian French, you begin to suspect that you are perhaps doing the same thing with your English. You begin to look on pronunciation in a more impartial, scientific, way. You will see that the dialect of your village or

town is not necessarily standard for other people!
You will, in fact, learn the virtues of modesty
and humility." (*The Student's Guide to Modern
Languages*.)

Poise and Harmony.

Here is suggestive comment on but a few of the
benefits that can accrue by the deliberate cultivation of an "abnormal liking for things foreign,"
but xenomania as with all the other manias and
isms has its dangers that should be avoided.

Poise and harmony need ever to be within
reach, though human frailty makes it impossible
for us to keep them always at hand. It would
be equally as foolish to extol all things foreign,
by doing less than justice to all things native, as
at present it is to enthrone wrong simply because
it is our own. As we shall never rid ourselves of
likes and dislikes, there is sound sense in endeavouring to rationalize them, ever remembering,
with Ruskin, that "What we lack determines
what we are, and is a sign of what we are," and
ever trying to recognize the good, the true, and
the beautiful, irrespective of their origin.

No. 25

YOUTHFULNESS

As we grow old we grow mature, but maturity is not necessarily the destroyer of youthfulness. We can grow old in years and older than our years in wisdom, and yet in spirit remain youthful. To be youthful we must be young, and there are more ways than one of being young. It is useless to fight against the passing of years, to refuse to listen to the voice of Father Time through the periods of childhood, adolescence, and adulthood. Each year can be made to enrich life, and the enrichment of life makes for happiness, which is often infused with the spirit of youthfulness. The voice is an authoritative voice that ultimately commands respect.

In childhood we heed it not. Indeed, during those days it is "a still small voice" that encourages us onward if we give ear to it. During adolescence we are still intent upon the future, still engaged upon the ascent. Our prime is not reached until we have lived through additional years during which the tendency is to flout rather than to fear the consequences of the march of time. Those years are seldom tinged with regrets that soon the descent must begin, but at last we have forced upon our physical selves the fact that we are not as we were, that Father Time is worthy of more attention than he has customarily received. Here in daily round is trite reminder of "the way of all flesh."

Spur and Check.

Casual observation as we walk about day by day furnishes us with abundant examples of the effects of time on all things that live, and death itself is evidence of life, without which the other could not happen. Always to be wise in our time and generation is an ideal that we can tightly grasp. Its attainment, however, over and over again escapes us. To strive to attain it acts both as spur and as check. Wisdom in youth impels us to do or to try to do things which, later, we shall be unable to do, and it also makes us refrain from doing things that are better avoided because of their evil effects that must be felt at a later stage in life.

Youthfulness is buoyant, but it need not be blind. It keeps close company with spontaneity and makes light of heavy responsibility—until freshness is tempered with discretion. Life and love and laughter trip lightly along in early years. We sing with Shakespeare—

What is love? 'Tis not hereafter;
Present mirth hath present laughter,

What's to come is still unsure :
In delay there lies no plenty ;
Then, come kiss me, sweet and twenty,
Youth's a stuff will not endure.

Because "Youth's a stuff will not endure,"
human nature makes the most of it. It uses it
unsparingly, and with excessive use there may be
abuse, of which we do not become fully conscious
until youth is "on the wing."

Action and Inactivity.

Youth is the time of great adventure. We are
all constituted differently. In terms of modern
psychology our complexes during the days of our
youth are rooted in problems of action rather than
of inactivity. Youth is restless, impatient, ambitious, desirous of change, now easily satisfied,
now just as easily dissatisfied. It is undiscriminating and yet ever critical. It is a spendthrift
of energy and yet never bankrupt, for mending
quickly follows spending, and the coffers are soon
replenished. If to-morrow is the subject of
thought, it is thought that is likely to be more
concerned with what can be done to add zest to
life to make life really worth while than with allure-
ments "the seer and yellow" suggest—quietude,
solitude, calmness, and serenity.

These truths and half-truths assume impressive
significance when youthfulness in relation to life

is thought of with the emphasis on the physical. They lose much of their impressiveness when spiritual values are uppermost in the mind. Undoubtedly, "Youth's a stuff will not endure"— physically. Some fail to reach three score years and ten.

Physical and Mental.

Physical youthfulness has passed to decay before the allotted span has run its course in some individuals and others go through the span as interesting examples of "young-old" men and women, but the limit of human life is short when counted in years and compared with the years of other forms of life. And with the decay of the physical comes a decline in the mental, notwithstanding "the ancients," who remain "in possession of all their faculties."

The mental faculty has its mainspring in the brain, which, of course, is part of the physical. Even the world's great men and women lose their powers of greatness as they continue to descend the mountain of life. The abnormal youthfulness of body and brain of George Bernard Shaw as he passed "the age limit" was extensively commented upon by journalists and others, but even this man of genius in his Metabiological Pentateuch, *Back to Methuselah*, the last section of which is entitled "As Far as Thought Can Reach"

187

("Summer afternoon in the year A.D. 31,920")
sounds a realistic note in his Preface: "I am not,
I hope, under more illusion than is humanly
inevitable as to the crudity of this my beginning
of a Bible for Creative Evolution. I am doing the
best I can at my age. My powers are waning;
but so much the better for those who found me
unbearably brilliant when I was in my prime."

Is it possible, then, to retain youthfulness in
life when Rise and Fall are so inexorable? Cynical
attitude towards life might couple youthfulness
with childishness, and suggest that many people,
although unable to prevent the growth of body,
admirably succeed in repressing the growth of
mind. Moreover, without being cynical or intellectually superior, it is possible to state in the
spirit of actuality that many men remain immature through life through lack of developmental
uses.

"Most people if asked to say what characterizes
the social life of the present day," points out Mr.
D. F. Fraser-Harris, M.D., D.Sc., F.R.S.E., in
*Coloured Thinking and Other Studies in Science
and Literature*, "would reply, the applications of
natural science to our pleasures and convenience;
and yet it is abundantly evident that along with
these notable and astounding developments of
science there is a very great deal of what can
only be described as childishness. If ever there

was an age when a rational view of knowledge seemed paramount it is the present, and yet co-existent with this there is a vast underlying substratum of the irrationality of the immature mind. The particular variety of mental immaturity of which we are thinking is the incapacity to grasp the universality of the doctrine of cause and effect. The *post hoc* is everywhere mistaken for the *propter hoc*, and this not only amongst the uneducated masses, but amongst those whose training should have disposed them to think far otherwise."

Life's Paradoxes.

Cannot youthfulness then, the common gift of Nature, be with us throughout life? Yes and no. No, when youthfulness is literally defined. There is "a time for everything," and the time for physical youthfulness is in early life. "Too old at forty," may be the cry of one age, and "young enough at sixty," may be the axiom of another age, and both may apply to physical life.

The mature life can see life in all its aspects. Professor A. R. Skemp, writing of art and temperament, pointed out that "the greatest artists disguise nothing and distort nothing; but, seeing wide as well as deep, they find balance and harmony in the whole. They see ugliness and beauty, joy and sorrow, cruelty and pity, terror and triumphant faith, weakness and strength—not isolated, but blended in infinite variety, and the greatest artists thus preserve in the revelation of each aspect of life the truth of a wider vision."

It is "the truth of a wider vision" that gives vitality to youth. Youthfulness is a spirit. It is the product of an attitude of mind. At fifty years of age we cannot do what was well within our physical powers at twenty-five, and at seventy-five we have to cope with greater physical handicaps than were experienced at fifty. But from the moment we reach the summit of the mountain of life and onwards for many years we can set against loss on the physical side gain on the mental side, and blend both the changing physical and the changing mental side to create qualities of the spirit that keep youthfulness alive. *Joie de vivre* has many expressions. Given maintenance of the right attitude towards the art of living during our allotted three score years and ten, we need not say good-bye to youthfulness of spirit before life itself says good-bye to us.

No. 26

ZEAL

ZEAL makes dynamic creatures of us all. It is the spur that makes action the sequel of thought. Unless we have zeal, we lack the spark that for many purposes is the only method of ignition. It is the feeling that crystallizes itself in personal activity. Zeal is a driving force. He can only believe in what he does, and do what he is impelled to do by the intensity of his belief. The man or woman with "a cause" is the man or woman of movement. To work for "a cause" is evidence that thought has been exercised, or that imagination has been fired, or that emotions have been effectually stimulated.

The pessimists of to-day—they are mostly of the older generation and, therefore, have the pre-War mentality, outlook, and interpretation of life—sometimes aver either that modern youth and maiden lack interest or that interest is wrongly centred. The zeal of former generations, they contend, is lacking. Few want to work, they say; all want to play, but in order to play they must have the means to purchase play, and these means can, in the majority of cases, be obtained only as the reward of labour. Owing, however, to the attitude adopted towards life in general and individual life in particular, there is excess of zeal in the pursuit of pleasure and lack of zeal in the performance of everyday duties that must be performed. The pessimists need not be followed farther along life's practical highway; with them there can be neither agreement nor disagreement without qualification unless truth be too severely strained.

Young and Old.

A pertinent point that emerges is that young and old are zealous in the ways that most strongly commend themselves. What is has always been. If the wisdom of age could always be stated to, and accepted by, youth, there would instantaneously be an end to many of the troubles that confront the average individual in the passage through life from youth to age. The ineradicable difficulty is that the wisdom of age derives its nurture from age itself, and that it is not more possible to make the young prematurely old than to make the old perpetually young, notwithstanding the extravagances of those zealots who see in the potentialities and potencies of thyroids and monkey glands the elixir not only of life but also of youthfulness.

These fundamental incompatabilities of interests, clashes of theories, and conflicts in practices should not, however, be made excuses for reminders that there is nothing to be gained by looking both backwards into the years that have passed and forwards into the years that are to come. There is much to be gained by comparison, which is the foundation of criticism. Reflection on these issues of life not only reveals differing senses of values, but also explains why different people are zealous in different causes. Their interests are differently rooted, though in educational training, intellectual capacity, and range of experience, there may be an absence of disparity to count for the differences.

An Accelerator of Activities.

Two members of one family, born of the same parents, given similar training, enjoying similar environmental influences, can grow up to think differently about many of the major issues in life, though both can be the possessors and reflectors of similar qualities of character. Zeal is expressive of differences. It is an accelerator of activities. Both interests and activities gain virility from the times in which we live. We have to make wrong discoveries, to find wrong purposes in life, and then by self-effort endeavour to bring them to complete fulfilment. "The personal struggle of recent times," Sir Flinders Petrie has stated, "has been to keep hold of one's own soul, to avoid being swept in as a mechanical cog in the wheels of 'progress.' The breathing places where Nature can be lived in are scantier every year. The hustle of life leaves less and less time really to live. One becomes more of a machine gauged by its output. It becomes more essential to go apart into a desert place where thinking-out can be done, where the rush of new impressions can be sorted over and built into one's personality, where the battle of prejudices and principles can be quietly concluded, and a new structure of assumptions accepted. It is useless to live into the 1930's if one lets one's being die at the 1910's. One must accept all that is true and widening in ideas, whatever one's youth was, but learn to skim off the dross and keep only the pure metal—sometimes very little of it remains."

Thinking Things Out.

This thinking out things for oneself is distasteful to many people in these days when attractions and distractions are so many, and when the selective principle is too often permitted to remain idle. Yet things require to be thought out, although zeal can be demonstrated haphazardly and without relationship to schematic treasure hunts for "the pure metal," which is the only kind of metal that is worth hunting for by those who are desirous of keeping themselves in the line of true progress. It is the exercise of thought that gives rise to conviction. We have to discover what we really want before we can be enthusiastic in our attempts to get it. Blind zeal can be as disastrous in result as deliberate wrong-doing. One of the most difficult tasks in life is for each individual to be true to himself or herself. External influences are powerful and diverse. The natural inclination to imitate has, upon occasions, to be resisted in order to avoid evil consequences. In short, there must be both thinking out and working out in the direction of self-realization.

Personal Bias.

We must know ourselves thoroughly before we can be ourselves, and both to know and to be are not as simple as they appear to be on the surface. "It often takes a long time for a sensitive, respectful youth to realize that he is one definite person and not an epitome of the human race," states Mr. J. W. N. Sullivan, in *Aspects of Science*. When the young man has learned for himself— ready knowledge is not the same for all—"he will," proceeds Mr. Sullivan, "no longer shrink from being classed as a man who 'knows what he likes.' His chief concern will be to find what it is he really does like, to stand by that and never to deny it. He will no longer be afraid of his personal bias. Santayana has said that there comes a time when a man realizes that all life for him has narrowed to one mortal career. A more important moment is when he realizes that he is one particular person. Both moments are realizations of limitations, but it is only after such moments that the man can achieve anything real. With the realization that one is not a catholic, receptive agent, with the realization that one is a limited but definite person, comes an entirely different attitude towards people and achievements. They are not now good or bad, judged by some impersonal standard; they are helps or hindrances. The academic classification may still, in a way, be accepted, but it is not a matter of vital interest. Life becomes dynamic, not static. Great names and great achievements become living, moribund, or dead—living or dead, that is to say, in relation to the principle of life that one feels within oneself."

Dynamic Forces.

There are dynamic forces in all of us. It is for each to discover for himself the best methods of liberation. "Zeal," says the dictionary, is "the compelling or passionate ardour for anything." Intensity is an excellent dynamic when it is securely harnessed to "something" that is both rightly understood and that is worthy. "Anything" is much too comprehensive. History has scores of lessons to teach in this connexion—one sound reason why retrospection is illuminating. Jerusalem was ruined in A.D. 70 because fanatics were zealous in their opposition to domination. Zeal can be most pointed in its aim and worthless when aim has been pressed to attainment. Right and wrong, good and bad, weak and strong, characterize both individual and collective endeavours. A practical point is that if "thinking-out" is well done on individual lines self-activity, self-revelation, and self-realization are likely to be best not only for self but for all with whom self associates.

Thought requires to be turned on the various aspects of self and to be expressed in conjunction with others, complete escape from whom, indeed, cannot be averted, for we cannot live as hermits and as members of a civilized community at one and the same time. Understanding of self, then, is of primary importance.

Responsibilities of Life.

"So soon as a person has developed a feeling of responsibility through the experience of his own initiative, it is possible to teach him," says Mr. L. H. Jones, A.M., in *Education as Growth*, "a sense of worthiness, as a result of meeting fairly and properly the responsibilities of life. This sense of worthiness as a result of right action is the noblest and most powerful motive that can be made to appeal to a human being. . . . Neither a sense of worth nor one of remorse can appeal to any person till he has had his sense of right and wrong somewhat developed, and this cannot be done with an individual till he appreciates to some extent his own power of initiative in action, and therefore his share of responsibility for the consequences of his action. Although all these appreciations develop in a sense together, yet there is a logical sequence which absolutely controls, however small, the portion of time intervening in any case."

Zeal, like all the other attributes of character, is expressive of quality. It is generated in the individual. Why and how it is used are conditioned by individual worth.

CONCLUSION

An alphabet of attributes in relation to adult
human life is as a box of bricks to the child. A
child plays as he can with the bricks that he
empties from the box. The adult is adaptable,
brave, charitable, determined, and so on through
the alphabet, an admixture of irrationality and
irresponsibilities. The child builds best when he
has mastered the principle of building. So it is
with the adult. To know which attribute is the
best for service at any given time, and, knowing,
to make use of it, is to exercise aright the most
difficult of all the arts—the art of true living. To
learn that art calls for zeal in many spheres of
human activity, and to be passionately arduous
as an exerciser of it is to be a zealot of the
best kind. The school in which the alphabet of
attributes is mastered is the world. It is the
school at which attendance is compulsory throughout life.

QUOTATIONS

AUTHORS

Adams, Sir John, 9, 104, 159
Addison, 95
Amiel, 67
Aristotle, 56
Aurelius, Marcus, 169
Barton, 94
Beaverbrook, Lord, 112, 116
Bennett, Arnold, 24
Bentham, Jeremy, 56, 77
Browning, Elizabeth Barrett, 109
Buddha, 136
Burnham, Dr. Wm. H., 154
Buxton, Fowle, 19
Cabanis, 96
Campagnac, E.T., 4, 31
Capek, 157
Carlyle, 150
Carncross, Dr. Horace, 35
Carr, Herbert W., 27
Cicero, 86
Confucius, 136
Coué, 59
Drinkwater, John, 140
Dryden, 32
Emerson, 98
Epictetus, 108
Epstein, 60
Firth, Violet M., 100
Fox, 131
Fraser-Harris, Dr. D. F., 188
Fuller, Sir Bampfylde, 37

Galsworthy, John, 62, 87, 117, 139, 149
Garnett, Edward, 105
Glover, W., 106, 110
Goethe, 94, 177
Haldane, Lord, 11, 23
Hamerton, P. G. 70, 97
Hazlitt, 117
Herbert, 76
Herbert, George, 72
Holmes, Edmond, 137
Hueffer, Ford Madox, 114
Hugon, Paul D., 60, 79
Huxley, T. H., 61
Joad, C. E. M., 56
Johnson, Samuel, 78
Jones, L. H., 197
Jones, W. Tudor, 133
Junius, 49
Kempis, Thomas à, 13
Locke, W. J., 174
Martin, Everett Dean, 52
Mason, J. W. T., 81
McDougall, Wm., 40, 67, 145
Mildmay, 118
Mill, John Stuart, 56
Morley, Lord, 6, 23, 122
Osgood, F. S., 75
Petrie, Sir Flinders, 193
Pope, 50
Rashdall, Rev. Hastings, 58
Raymond, Ernest, 55
Read, Herbert, 59, 63
Richards, I. A., 17

14B—(2088)

AUTHORS—(*contd.*)

Robinson, James Harvey, 160
Rochefoucauld, 165
Ruskin, John, 183
Schlegel, 152
Schopenhauer, 170
Scott, Walter, 62, 138
Shakespeare, William, 61, 83, 185
Shaw, George Bernard, 60, 89, 178, 187
Skemp, A. R., 189

Smiles, Samuel, 76
Stevenson, R. L., 62
Stoddard, Lothrop, 14, 146
Sullivan, J. W. N., 195
Swift, Edgar James, 1
Theognis, 93
Tracey, A. G., 62
Turner, J. E., 125
Weir, Archibald, 18
Wells, H. G., 62, 179
Whitby, Dr. Charles J., 163
Wilson, P. G., 181

BOOKS

Addresses and Essays, 11
Aspects of Science, 195
Back to Methuselah, 178, 187
Causes and Consequences, 37
Character and the Conduct of Life 40, 67, 145
Coloured Thinking and Other Studies in Science and Literature, 188
Creative Freedom, 81
Education, 4, 31
Education as Growth, 197
Educational Theories 9, 159
Know Your Own Mind, 106
Machinery of the Mind, 100
Makers of Man, 163
Morals of Marcus Ordeyne, 174
On Compromise, 122
Othello, 66
Others, 18
Our Minds and Our Motives, 60, 79, 128
Oxford English Dictionary, 174
Personality and Reality, 125
Plain Living and High Thinking, 47

Practical Criticism, 17
Psychology 52
Reason and Romanticism, 59
R.U.R., 157
Scientific Humanism, 14, 146
Self-Realization, 137
Success, 112
The Appreciation of Literature, 62
The Critical Attitude, 114
The Escape from the Primitive, 35
The Freewill Problem, 27
The Humanizing of Knowledge, 160
The Intellectual Life, 70, 97
The Island Pharisees, 117
The Normal Mind, 154
The Pigeon, 149
The Secret of Success, 16
The Spiritual Ascent of Man, 133
The Student's Guide to Modern Languages, 183
The World of William Clissold, 179
Three Plays for Puritans, 89
Through Literature to Life, 55